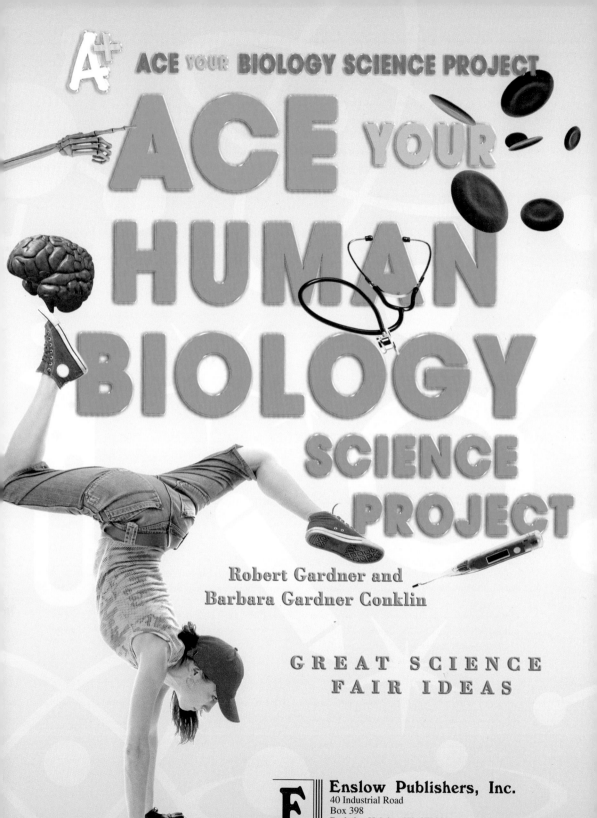

ACE YOUR BIOLOGY SCIENCE PROJECT

ACE YOUR HUMAN BIOLOGY SCIENCE PROJECT

Robert Gardner and
Barbara Gardner Conklin

GREAT SCIENCE
FAIR IDEAS

Enslow Publishers, Inc.
40 Industrial Road
Box 398
Berkeley Heights, NJ 07922
USA

http://www.enslow.com

Library of Congress Cataloging-in-Publication Data

Gardner, Robert, 1929–
     Ace your human biology science project : great science fair ideas / Robert Gardner and Barbara
        Gardner Conklin.
          p. cm. — (Ace your biology science project)
     Includes bibliographical references and index.
     Summary: "Presents several science projects and science project ideas about human biology"—
        Provided by publisher.
     ISBN-13: 978-0-7660-3219-4
     ISBN-10: 0-7660-3219-1
     1. Human biology—Experiments—Juvenile literature. 2. Science projects—Juvenile literature.
        3. Science fairs—Juvenile literature. I. Conklin, Barbara Gardner. II. Title.
     QP37.G358 2010
     612—dc22
                                                          2008030799

Printed in the United States of America

10 9 8 7 6 5 4 3 2 1

To Our Readers: We have done our best to make sure all Internet Addresses in this book were active and appropriate when we went to press. However, the author and the publisher have no control over and assume no liability for the material available on those Internet sites or on other Web sites they may link to. Any comments or suggestions can be sent by e-mail to comments@enslow.com or to the address on the back cover.

♻ Enslow Publishers, Inc., is committed to printing our books on recycled paper. The paper in every book contains 10% to 30% post-consumer waste (PCW). The cover board on the outside of each book contains 100% PCW. Our goal is to do our part to help young people and the environment too!

The experiments in this book are a collection of the authors' best experiments, which were previously published by Enslow Publishers, Inc., in *Health Science Projects About Heredity*, *Health Science Projects About Sports Performance*, *Health Science Projects About Anatomy and Physiology*, *Health Science Projects About Nutrition*, and *Health Science Projects About Psychology*.

Illustration Credits: © bubaone/iStockphoto.com, trophy icons; © Chen Fu Soh/iStockphoto.com, backgrounds; © Chris Schmidt/iStockphoto.com, p. 106; Enslow Publishers, Inc., Figures 4, 7, 13a, 24–27, 29; Life Art image copyright 1998 Lippincott Williams & Wilkins, Figures 1–3, 5, 8, 11, 12, 13b, 15, 17, 19; Shutterstock, pp. 1, 10, 62; Stephen F. Delisle, Figures 6, 9, 10, 14, 16, 18, 20–23, 28, 30, 31.

Cover Photos: Shutterstock

CONTENTS

The Human Body

CHAPTER 2

The Circulatory, Respiratory, and Digestive Systems

The Nervous and Endocrine Systems

🕐 *Experiments marked with this symbol contain material that might be used for a science fair project.*

○ **Experiments marked with this symbol contain material that might be used for a science fair project.**

INTRODUCTION

When you hear the word *science*, do you think of a person in a white lab coat surrounded by beakers of bubbling liquids, specialized lab equipment, and computers? What exactly is science? Maybe you think science is only a subject you learn in school. Science is much more than this.

Science is the study of the things that are all around you, every day. No matter where you are or what you are doing, scientific principles are at work. You don't need special materials, equipment, or even a white lab coat to be a scientist. Materials commonly found in your home, at school, or at a local store will allow you to become a scientist and pursue an area of interest. By making careful observations and asking questions about how things work, you can begin to design experiments to investigate a variety of questions. You can do science. You probably already have but just didn't know it!

Perhaps you are reading this book because you are looking for an idea for a science fair project for school, or maybe you are just hoping to find something fun to do on a rainy day. This book will provide an opportunity to conduct experiments and collect data to learn more about human biology.

SCIENCE FAIRS

Many of the experiments in this book may be appropriate for science fair projects. Experiments marked with an asterisk (⦿) include a section called Science Fair Project Ideas. The ideas in this section will provide suggestions to help you develop your own original science fair project. However, judges at such fairs do not reward projects or experiments that are simply copied from a book. For example, a model of a human cell or organ, which is commonly found at these fairs, would probably not impress judges unless it was done in a novel way. On the other hand, a carefully performed experiment to find out how exercise affects carbon dioxide output would be likely to receive careful consideration.

THE SCIENTIFIC METHOD

All scientists look at the world and try to understand how things work. They make careful observations and conduct research about a question. Different areas of science use different approaches. Depending on the phenomenon being investigated, one method is likely to be more appropriate than another. Designing a new medication for heart disease, studying the spread of an invasive plant species such as purple loosestrife, and finding evidence that there was once water on Mars all require different methods.

Despite the differences, however, all scientists use a similar general approach to do experiments. It is called the scientific method. In most experiments, some or all of the following steps are used: making an observation, formulating a question, making a hypothesis (an answer to the question) and a prediction (an if-then statement), designing and conducting an experiment, analyzing results and drawing conclusions about your prediction, and accepting or rejecting the hypothesis. Scientists then share their findings with others by writing articles that are published in journals. After—and only after—a hypothesis has repeatedly been supported by experiments can it be considered a theory.

You might be wondering how to get an experiment started. When you observe something in the world, you may become curious and think of a question. Your question can be answered by a well-designed investigation. Your question may also arise from an earlier experiment or from background reading. Once you have a question, you should make a hypothesis. Your hypothesis is a possible answer to the question (what you think will happen). Once you have a hypothesis, it is time to design an experiment.

In most cases, it is appropriate to do a controlled experiment. This means there are two groups treated exactly the same except for the single factor that you are testing. That factor is often called a variable. For example, if you want to investigate whether exercise affects heart rate, two groups may be used. One group is called the control group, and the other is called the experimental group. The two groups of people should be treated exactly the same. The people in the control group will sit quietly for five minutes while the people in the experimental group will jog in place for five minutes. The variable is exercise—it is the thing that changes, and it is the only difference between the two groups.

During the experiment, you will collect data. For example, you will measure heart rate after the period of five minutes of either rest or exercise. You might also note how quickly each person is breathing and the color of each person's face. By comparing the data collected from the control group with the data collected from the experimental group, you will draw conclusions. Since the two groups were treated exactly alike except for exercising, an increase in heart rate of the people in the experimental group would allow you to conclude with confidence that increased heart rate is a result of the one thing that was different: exercise.

Two other terms that are often used in scientific experiments are *dependent* and *independent* variables. One dependent variable here is heart rate, because it depends upon exercise. Exercise is the independent variable (it doesn't depend on anything). After the data is collected, it is analyzed to see whether the hypothesis was supported or rejected. Often, the results of one experiment will lead you to a related question, or they may send you off in a different direction. Whatever the results, there is something to be learned from all scientific experiments.

SCIENCE PROJECTS

Science fair judges tend to reward creative thought and imagination. It helps if you are really interested in your project. Take the time to choose a topic that really appeals to you. Consider, too, your own ability and the cost of materials. Don't pursue a project that you can't afford.

If you decide to use a project found in this book for a science fair, you will need to find ways to modify or extend it. This should not be difficult because you will probably find that as you do these projects new ideas for experiments will come to mind. These new experiments could make excellent science fair projects, particularly because they spring from your own mind and are interesting to you.

If you decide to enter a science fair and have never done so before, you should read some of the books listed in the Further Reading section. The books that deal specifically with science fairs will provide plenty of helpful hints and lots of useful information that will enable you to avoid the pitfalls that sometimes plague first-time entrants. You will learn how to prepare appealing reports that include charts and graphs, how to set up and display your work, how to present your project, and how to relate to judges and visitors.

SAFETY FIRST

As with many activities, safety is important in science, and certain rules apply when conducting experiments. Some of the rules below may seem obvious to you, while others may not, but each is important to follow.

1. Have **an adult** help you whenever the book advises.

2. Wear eye protection and closed-toe shoes (rather than sandals), and tie back long hair.

3. Don't eat or drink while doing experiments, and never taste substances being used (unless instructed to do so).

4. Avoid touching chemicals.

5. When doing these experiments, use only nonmercury thermometers, such as those filled with alcohol. The liquid in some thermometers is mercury. It is dangerous to breathe mercury vapor. If you have

mercury thermometers, **ask an adult** to take them to a local mercury thermometer exchange location.

6. When using a microscope, always use indirect lighting when illuminating objects. Never use the microscope mirror to capture direct sunlight. Because the mirror concentrates light rays, you could permanently damage your eyes.

7. Do only those experiments that are described in the book or those that have been approved by **an adult**.

8. Never engage in horseplay or play practical jokes.

9. Before beginning, read through the entire experimental procedure to make sure you understand all instructions, and clear all extra items from your work space.

10. At the end of every activity, clean all materials used and put them away. Wash your hands thoroughly with soap and water.

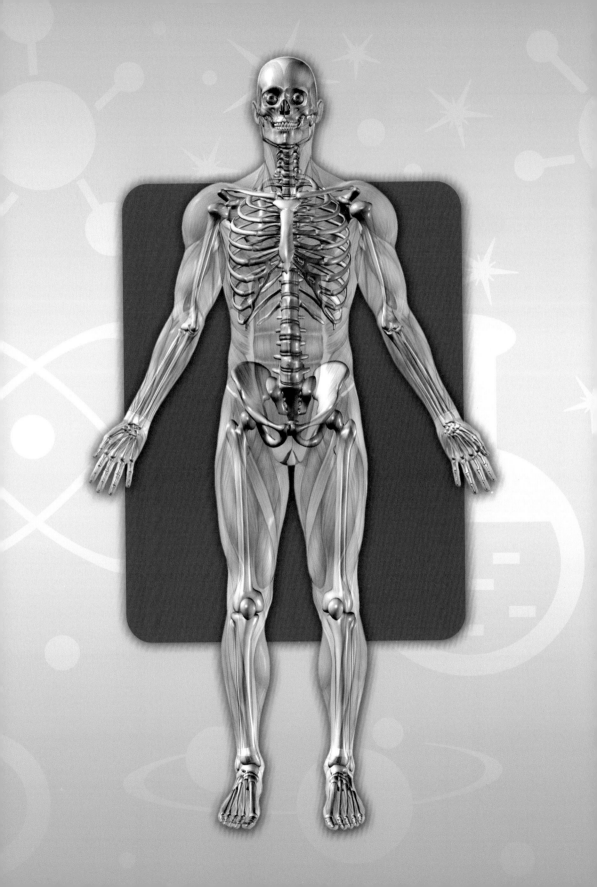

Chapter 1

The Human Body

ALL HUMANS BELONG TO THE SAME SPECIES: *HOMO SAPIENS*. As *Homo sapiens*, we share many features. We have all the characteristics of mammals and of primates. Like all primates, our teeth are adapted to a general diet, and our eyes are at the front of our heads so that each eye has the same view from a slightly different angle. This eye placement gives us a three-dimensional view of the world and therefore good depth perception. The upper sides of our fingers and toes are covered by flat nails rather than claws. Our fingers and toes are flexible and capable of a wide range of movement.

We also differ from other primates in some ways. Our big toes are not opposable (they cannot touch the other toes) and are not splayed (turned out) as they are in most primates. But our thumbs are almost as long as our other digits (fingers). This allows us to grip and manipulate tools with great precision. We walk on two feet, not four. Finally, our brains are three times as large as those of chimpanzees—our closest primate relatives. Our big brains enable us to make extensive use of language, the basis for human culture.

The human body is made up of nearly a hundred trillion (100,000,000,000,000) cells. There are hundreds of different types of cells, clustered into five kinds of tissue: muscle, nerve, blood,

[FIGURE 1]

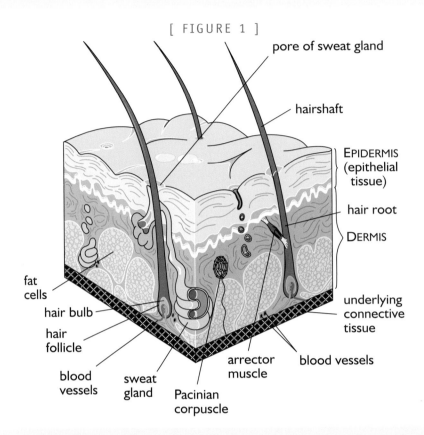

pore of sweat gland

hairshaft

EPIDERMIS
(epithelial
tissue)

hair root

DERMIS

fat
cells

hair bulb

hair
follicle

blood
vessels

sweat
gland

Pacinian
corpuscle

arrector
muscle

blood vessels

underlying
connective
tissue

This small section of skin is greatly magnified. The Pacinian corpuscle responds to pressure by generating nerve impulses.

connective (which supports or covers organs), and epithelial (which covers or lines other tissues).

Your skin is a protective cover of epidermal cells (epithelial tissue) that blankets a layer of connective tissue known as the dermis. Dermis cells anchor the skin to underlying connective tissue, muscles, and bones. Within the dermis are blood vessels, nerve cells, sweat glands, and hair follicles (see Figure 1). Fingernails, toenails, and hair grow out of the skin.

Your skin provides protection from infection, drying out, harmful rays, and injury. It is essential in regulating body temperature, and it contains a variety of sensory organs that respond to touch, pressure, temperature, and pain. Because water and salts are lost through the skin, it also serves a role in excreting body wastes.

1.1 How Does Skin Help Regulate Body Temperature?

Materials:
- eyedropper
- alcohol
- water
- waxed paper
- socks
- fan

As you know, exercise can make you sweat. To see how sweat helps to regulate your body temperature, use an eyedropper to place a few drops of alcohol and an equal number of water drops on a piece of waxed paper. Which liquid disappears (evaporates) first?

Now place the same number of drops of each liquid on your forearm. Spread the drops out over your skin. Which liquid makes your skin feel cooler?

On a warm, dry (not humid) day, put a dry sock on one foot and a sock you have dipped in warm water on the other. After several minutes, which foot feels cooler? Can you explain why it feels cooler? Do you detect any change if you place both feet in front of a fan?

Science Fair Project Ideas

- Design and carry out an experiment to see how temperature affects the rate at which water evaporates.
- The skin on your fingertips has friction ridges. If you look closely, you can see them. Design a technique to record fingerprints. Then collect fingerprints from a number of people. Can you find any two sets of fingerprints that are the same?
- How do detectives lift fingerprints from a surface?
- Investigate the use of fingerprints in forensic science.

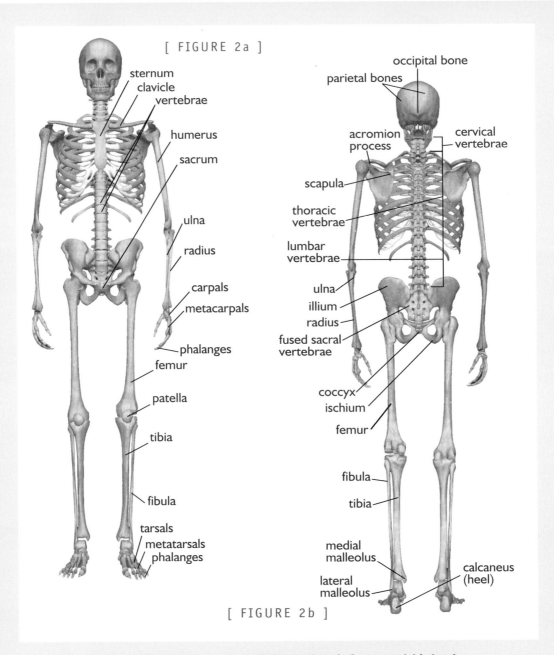

sternum
clavicle
vertebrae

humerus

sacrum

ulna

radius

carpals

metacarpals

phalanges
femur

patella

tibia

fibula

tarsals
metatarsals
phalanges

occipital bone

parietal bones

acromion
process

cervical
vertebrae

scapula

thoracic
vertebrae

lumbar
vertebrae

ulna
illium
radius

fused sacral
vertebrae

coccyx
ischium

femur

fibula

tibia

medial
malleolus

lateral
malleolus

calcaneus
(heel)

[FIGURE 2b]

The human skeleton as seen from the a) front and b) back.

YOUR SKELETON

A house has a hidden frame to which everything else is attached. Your body is similar. Beneath your skin and flesh lies the frame—the bony skeleton—to which your body is attached. Although the bones of an adult weigh only about nine kilograms (twenty pounds), they provide a sound framework because they are stronger than reinforced concrete.

Bones are more than a frame; they enclose and protect your brain, spinal cord, and other organs. The marrow inside bones produces the red blood cells that carry oxygen and the white blood cells that help you combat infections.

You were born with more than three hundred separate bones. By the time you are an adult, that number will be just a few more than two hundred, because many of the separate bones fuse together.

Figure 2a is a frontal view of the major bones that make up an adult skeleton. Figure 2b is a rear view of that skeleton.

The skeleton is divided into two parts. The axial skeleton consists of the skull, vertebrae (backbone), ribs, and sternum. The bones attached to the axial skeleton—the arms, legs, scapula, clavicle, and pelvis—constitute the appendicular skeleton.

Bones are held together and connected by ligaments. Muscles, which are connected to your bones by tendons, enable you to move some of your bones. The points about which your bones move relative to one another are called joints.

Materials:

-a partner, preferably one who is thin so you can easily feel his or her bones

You cannot see the bones in your body. They are covered with muscles, connective tissue, and skin.

Even though you cannot see your bones, you can feel many of them. Your skull, for example, feels like one large bone. It is actually a number of separate bones that have fused or are fusing (see Figure 3). The gaps that existed between your skull bones when you were a baby allowed your brain to grow. That is necessary because at birth human brains are only one-third their adult size. During its first year, the average baby's brain grows from 400 g (14 oz.) to 990 g (35 oz.). By age six or seven, a child's brain is fully grown (1300 g or 46 oz.), which is why a child's head appears to be too large for its body.

The three bones of the middle ear (hammer, anvil, and stirrup) move when the eardrum vibrates. The only other bone in your head that moves is your mandible, or lower jaw. It moves when you talk or chew. Your lower teeth are embedded in your mandible. The front part of the mandible constitutes your chin.

MANDIBLE

Beginning at your chin, feel back along one side of your mandible. You will find that the rear end of the mandible turns upward at almost a right angle to articulate (form a joint) with the rest of the skull. The bone is connected to other bones of the head by ligaments. Tendons connect the mandible to muscles that make it move.

CLAVICLE, STERNUM, AND SCAPULA

At the base of your neck, on either side, you can feel the clavicle (collarbone). You will find that it extends laterally (sideways) on both sides. Near the center of your upper chest it connects with your sternum.

Skeleton

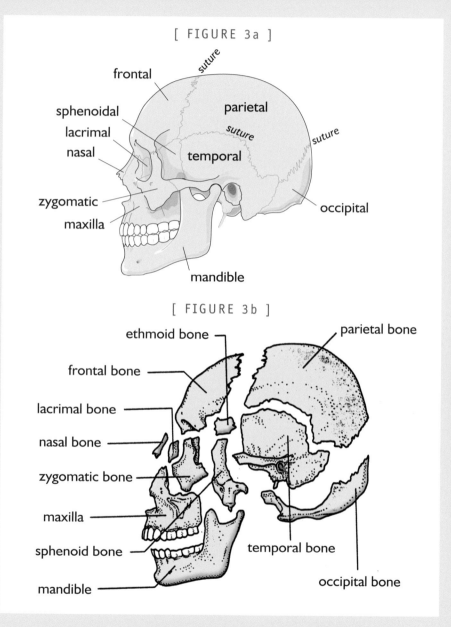

[FIGURE 3a]

frontal

suture

sphenoidal

lacrimal

nasal

parietal

suture

suture

temporal

zygomatic

occipital

maxilla

mandible

[FIGURE 3b]

ethmoid bone

parietal bone

frontal bone

lacrimal bone

nasal bone

zygomatic bone

maxilla

sphenoid bone

temporal bone

mandible

occipital bone

The human skull showing a) side view and b) individual bones that make up the skull.

You can feel the outer side of the sternum (breastbone). It runs down the center of your chest toward your abdomen. It narrows at its lower end to form a slightly pointed structure known as the xiphoid process. The outer end of your clavicle connects with the scapula (shoulder blade).

Feel a friend's scapula. It has a ridge, called the spine, which ends at the acromion process. It is the part of the shoulder farthest from the middle of the body. Below the acromion process is a concave depression known as the glenoid cavity.

ARM, WRIST, AND HAND

The rounded end of the humerus (upper arm bone) fits into and can rotate in the glenoid cavity. You can feel the shaft of your humerus at the center of your upper arm. But the upper end lies under the acromion process and muscle tissue. You will find that the lower end of the humerus is wide and articulates with the two bones of the lower arm.

What we normally call the elbow, or funny bone, is the upper end of the ulna. If you follow the ulna downward, you will find that it ends in the knobby styloid process above the little-finger side of the wrist.

The styloid process of the other bone of the lower arm—the radius—can be found above the thumb side of the wrist. You can follow the radius upward to the point where it articulates with the humerus.

The wrist is made up of eight small bones called the carpals, which are difficult to identify individually. You can, however, feel the five metacarpal bones on the back of your hand. The lower ends of these bones articulate with the phalanges, or fingers. There are a total of fourteen phalanges on each hand. Three are found in each finger and two in the thumb. The joints where metacarpals and phalanges meet are commonly known as your knuckles.

As you can see in Figure 4, many mammals have the same arm bones, even though their relative sizes and functions vary greatly. Such structures are said to be homologous: The bones have the same origin and basic structure even though they serve different purposes.

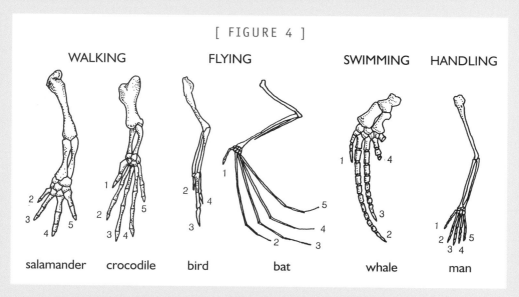

[FIGURE 4]

WALKING   FLYING   SWIMMING   HANDLING

salamander   crocodile   bird   bat   whale   man

These forelimbs are homologous. What differences do you see? What do the numbers indicate?

BACK AND RIBS

The skull sits atop the thirty-three bones that make up the vertebral column. There are seven cervical vertebrae in the neck, twelve thoracic vertebrae at the rear of the chest, and five lumbar vertebrae in the lower back. By adulthood, the five sacral vertebrae and four coccygeal vertebrae fuse with one another and with the pelvis. The fused sacral vertebrae are referred to as the sacrum. The fused coccygeal vertebrae are called the coccyx. In many animals the coccygeal vertebrae are separate and more numerous. They are the bones that lie within an animal's tail.

The vertebral column encloses and protects the spinal cord—the body's major nerve cells that connect the brain with the muscles and sensory cells of the body below the head. Many of the vertebrae have spinal processes that you can feel if you run your fingers along a friend's backbone. The thoracic vertebrae also have transverse processes that articulate with the twelve ribs on each side of the body, which you can also feel.

The ribs surround the lungs and heart, which lie within the upper body's thoracic cavity. You can trace the path of one or more of the ribs from a thoracic vertebrae on the back to the sternum at the front of the body. The lower two ribs are called floating ribs. They do not attach to the sternum. The three pairs of ribs above the floaters join together to form a common band of cartilage that attaches to the sternum beside the xiphoid process. The remaining seven pairs of ribs end in cartilage that connect them directly to the sternum. At least part of each of these upper seven pairs of ribs lies under the scapula, so it is difficult to trace these ribs all the way from vertebra to sternum.

PELVIS, LEGS, AND FEET

The pelvis, shown in Figure 5, is similar in some ways to the shoulders. Just as the arms articulate with the shoulder bones, so the legs articulate with the pelvis. The rear of the pelvis is fused with the sacral and coccygeal vertebrae. It feels like a solid plate that covers the lower part of the back. The sides of the pelvis are formed by the ilium bones (hipbones) that you can feel on either side of your belly. The bottom of the pelvis consists of the ischium bones, the bones you sit on. The pubis bones form the front of the pelvis. They join to form the pubic symphysis at the middle of the very lowest part of your abdomen. You can feel them on either side of your body at the base of your groin.

The femur (upper leg bone) is the longest bone in your body. The rounded head at its upper end fits into a concavity in the pubis. You can feel the outer upper end of the femur move as you walk. Feel, too, the very wide lower end of your femur. It lies behind your patella (kneecap).

The lower end of the femur articulates with the tibia (shinbone), the larger of the two bones of the lower leg. You can feel the entire front side of the tibia. Start just below the patella and follow it to its bulblike end on the inner (medial) side of your leg beside the ankle. The bulblike end of the tibia, the medial malleolus, has its complement on the other side of the ankle—the lateral malleolus. However, the

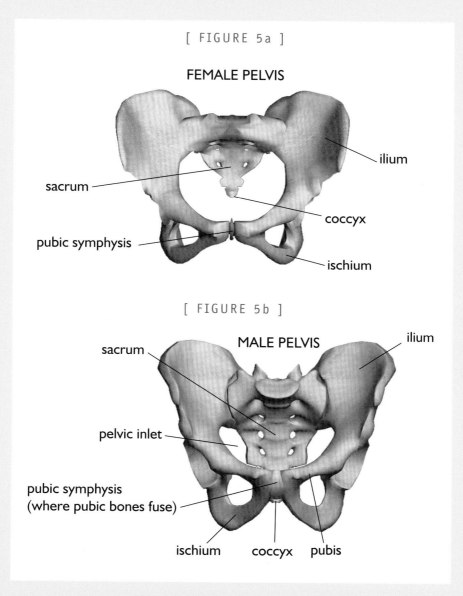

FEMALE PELVIS

ilium

sacrum

coccyx

pubic symphysis

ischium

[FIGURE 5b]

MALE PELVIS

ilium

sacrum

pelvic inlet

pubic symphysis
(where pubic bones fuse)

ischium   coccyx   pubis

The female pelvis (a) is wider and shallower than the male pelvis (b). Both, however, have the same bones. They are simply slightly different in shape.

lateral malleolus is the lower end of the fibula, which lies on the outer (lateral) side of your leg. How far can you trace the fibula up your leg?

Like the wrist, the ankle consists of a number of bones—the tarsals, of which there are seven. The largest tarsal bone is the heel bone or calcaneus, which you can feel on the lower rear portion of your foot.

The metatarsals lie between the toes and the ankle and correspond to the metacarpals in the hand. You can probably feel all five of your metatarsals by moving your fingers over the top of your foot behind your toes.

The front ends of the metatarsals articulate with the phalanges, commonly known as toes. Each foot, like your hands, has a total of fourteen phalanges. There are three phalanges in each of the four smaller toes and two in the great (big) toe.

You have now examined as many of the bones from your head to your toes as you can feel. Which bones were you not able to feel?

Science Fair Project Ideas

- On a real or plastic model of a human skeleton, or on detailed anatomical diagrams, identify all of the bones found in a human adult.
- Police often ask anthropologists to examine skeletal remains at crime scenes. Why do police ask anthropologists to examine skeletons? How do anthropologists distinguish between male and female skeletons?
- Visit a science museum where the skeletons of different animals are on display. Can you identify bones similar to those found in humans in the bodies of these other animals?
- Broken bones—fractures—are common injuries. What are the various types of fractures and how are they treated?

1.3 How Do Joints Work?

Materials:
-a partner, preferably one who is thin so you can easily feel his or her bones
-3 soda straws
-scissors
-string

The places where different bones articulate are called joints. Having examined the various bones of your body, you know that not all joints are the same.

FIXED JOINTS

Some of your joints are fixed. They do not allow movement. The bones of your skull, which were separate and distinct at birth, become fused with time. The lines along which they join are known as sutures. Fixed joints are also found in many bones of the face.

SLIGHTLY MOVABLE JOINTS

The ends of bones that have limited movement at a joint are generally padded with cartilage or joined by slightly flexible ligaments. The lower ends of the tibia and fibula are joined by such ligaments so that these two bones may undergo slight movement with respect to one another.

The cartilage between the bones of the pelvis allows slight movement. Between the vertebrae that make up your backbone, there are disks of cartilage that permit twisting, compression, and extension. The movement between adjacent vertebrae is limited. However, because there are many vertebrae, your back has considerable flexibility. Through approximately what angle can you bend your back forward? Backward?

To see how many vertebrae make flexibility possible even though movement between any two is limited, try this experiment. Take two soda straws. Cut one straw into ten or twelve pieces. Leave the other straw whole. Run a length of string through each straw.

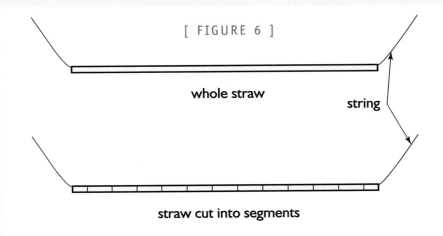

[FIGURE 6]

whole straw

string

straw cut into segments

A straw cut into many segments can serve as a model of the vertebrae that make up your backbone. The cut-up straw and the uncut one are both suspended on strings. How do the two compare with regard to flexibility?

Hold the ends of each straw as shown in Figure 6. Which straw provides greater flexibility?

To see why it is advantageous to have many vertebrae, cut a third straw into three pieces and run a string through it. How does its flexibility compare with the straw that has ten or twelve segments?

MOVABLE JOINTS

Most joints in your body are movable, but some provide a greater range of movement than others. The ends of bones in movable joints are covered by cartilage, and a membrane-enclosed fluid (synovial fluid) lies between them. The fluid serves as a lubricant for joints.

PIVOT JOINTS

A pivot joint allows one bone to rotate on another in much the same way that a faucet turns. You can turn your head, as in shaking your head to indicate no, because of a pivot joint. The first two cervical vertebrae—the atlas (first) and the axis (second)—form this pivot joint. The long vertical process of the axis fits into an opening in the anterior (front) side of the atlas (see Figure 7). This allows the atlas, which is firmly attached to the head, to turn (pivot) right or left on the axis.

You can also turn your palm forward or backward by twisting your forearm because of another pivot joint. If your arm is very thin, you may be able to feel the radius turn as you turn your palm. The radius turns on a concave notch on the ulna on the inside of the elbow.

HINGE JOINTS

Hinge joints are so named because they allow bones to move in the same way that a door swings on its hinges. A door's hinge allows it to swing nearly 180 degrees, but no farther. Straighten your arm. Then bend it slowly. Which bones move? Is the joint between your humerus and ulna a hinge joint? Why is the joint between your femur and tibia at your knee a hinge joint? Where else in your body can you find hinge joints?

BALL-AND-SOCKET JOINTS

When the sphere-shaped end of one bone fits into a cuplike cavity in another bone, you have a ball-and-socket joint. Such a joint allows movement in many directions, and it allows rotation. The joint at your shoulder where the end of the humerus fits into the scapula's glenoid cavity provides you with your most mobile joint. In how many different directions can you move your upper arm? Can you rotate it in a complete circle?

Your other ball-and-socket joint is the articulation of your femur and pelvis. In how many directions can you move your upper leg? Why is it not as mobile as your shoulder joint?

CONDYLOID JOINTS

A condyloid joint is one in which the oval-shaped end (condyle) of one bone fits into the elliptical cavity of another. The radius and one of the carpal

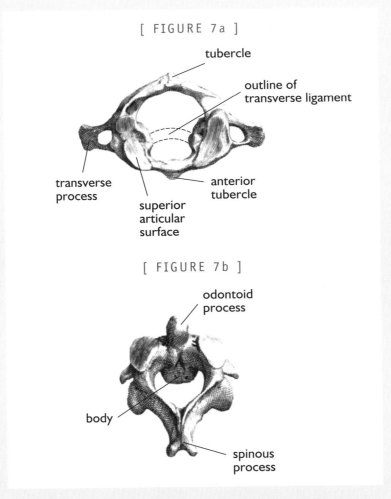

[FIGURE 7a]

tubercle

outline of
transverse ligament

transverse
process

anterior
tubercle

superior
articular
surface

[FIGURE 7b]

odontoid
process

body

spinous
process

7a) A top view of the atlas, or first cervical vertebra (C-1).
b) A side view of the axis, or second cervical vertebra (C-2).
The odontoid process fits into the opening in front of the
transverse ligament of the atlas. The atlas, which supports
the skull's occipital bone, turns about the odontoid process.

bones behind your thumb form a condyloid joint at your wrist. What kind of motion does this type of joint allow?

SADDLE JOINTS

In a saddle joint, the two bones that articulate both have convex and concave surfaces that mesh. The only saddle joints in your body are the joints formed by the metacarpal bones behind your thumbs and one of the carpal bones in your wrist. Use one of your thumbs to find out what kind of motions a saddle joint allows.

GLIDING JOINTS

A gliding joint, as its name implies, allows bones to glide over one another. Bones that meet in a gliding joint have nearly flat surfaces. Such joints are found between carpal and tarsal bones and between vertebrae. Can you detect the motion of any gliding joints with your fingers?

 Science Fair Project Ideas

- What is the origin of the terms *atlas* and *axis* for the first two cervical vertebrae?
- A person's weight while standing can squeeze joints together, particularly the vertebral joints. Could such squeezing change a person's height during the course of a day? Design and carry out an experiment to find out.
- Often, when you bend your knees, raise your arm, or crack your knuckles, you hear a snapping sound. What causes such a sound?
- People who can contort their limbs and phalanges well beyond the normal range of flexibility are often said to be double-jointed. Are they really double-jointed?

MUSCLES: THE PRIME MOVERS

All motions of your body, visible and invisible, are made possible by muscles. In addition to running, walking, and jumping, there are motions within your body that take place even when you are asleep. Your heart contracts about once every second throughout your life. You breathe because muscles move your ribs and diaphragm up and down. There are also muscles, of which you are totally unaware, that move food and fluids along your stomach and intestines or blood through your blood vessels. With so much to do, it is not surprising that muscles account for nearly half your weight.

All muscle tissue possesses irritability, contractility, extensibility, and elasticity. *Irritability* means that a muscle will respond to nerve impulses. *Contractility* is its ability to contract, to become shorter and thicker. Such contraction can cause a bone to move. *Extensibility* means that muscle tissue can be stretched or extended by a force. *Elasticity* means that a muscle, like a rubber band, resumes its original size after being extended.

Muscles are made up of many elongated cells known as fibers that are held together by connective tissue. There are three types of muscle tissue. Striated muscle, when viewed through a microscope, has stripes across its cells. It is the type of muscle that makes bones move. It is also called voluntary muscle because you can control its action. The biceps muscle on your upper arm is a striated or voluntary muscle. You decide voluntarily to contract that muscle and thereby lift your forearm. Nonstriated or smooth muscles are also known as involuntary muscles because you cannot control, nor are you consciously aware of, their action. You may, however, hear the results of their contraction. The gurgling sounds in your abdomen are the result of smooth muscle contractions around your stomach and intestines that cause fluids to move.

The third type of muscle—cardiac muscle—is found only in the heart. Its fibers have striations, but they are less distinct than in skeletal muscle, and the cells are smaller. The heart acts as one large muscle. When it contracts, it squeezes blood from the heart into two major arteries that lead to all parts of the body.

In experiments involving single muscle fibers, scientists use an electric current as a stimulus. The results of such experiments show that when the current reaches sufficient strength (minimal stimulus), the fiber will contract its maximum amount. Increasing the strength of the stimulus has no effect on the contraction, and any stimulus less than minimal will have no effect. This is known as the all-or-none law. Each muscle cell gives its maximum response or none at all.

In an ordinary muscle contraction, many fibers are stimulated. The total force exerted by the muscle depends on the number of fibers that contract. If you use a muscle to raise the maximum load it can lift, all the fibers in the muscle will contract. In most muscle activity, only a fraction of the fibers contract at any one time. To avoid fatigue, some fibers will contract while others relax.

Materials:

-an adult

-chicken wing
 (uncooked)

-newspapers

-sharp knife

-tweezers

-scissors

-probe, such as a
 slender stick
 or finishing nail

To play sports, or do anything for that matter, we move by using our muscles. The major muscles found in the human body are shown in Figure 8.

How do muscles work? Why do they sometimes not work? By dissecting a chicken wing, you will see what muscles look like and how they connect to bones.

Obtain an uncooked chicken wing from a meat market. Place the wing on some newspaper, and **ask an adult to help you cut it apart.** You will need a sharp knife, a pair of tweezers, scissors, and a probe (a stick or finishing nail can serve as a probe). Most of the skin can be pulled away with your fingers. As you pull away the skin, notice the connective tissue that connects it to the muscles beneath it.

Notice that each muscle is covered by a very thin transparent membrane. With tweezers and a probe, separate the muscles from one another. See if you can find where each muscle attaches to a bone. The muscles are attached to bones by tough, white, fibrous tendons. Pull on each muscle to see how its contraction makes a bone move.

Using scissors, cut the tendons and remove the muscles so you can see the bones. As Figure 9 shows, the major bones in a chicken wing are very similar to your arm bones. Can you find the humerus? The radius? The ulna? How do the carpals, metacarpals, and phalanges of a chicken's "arm" differ from yours?

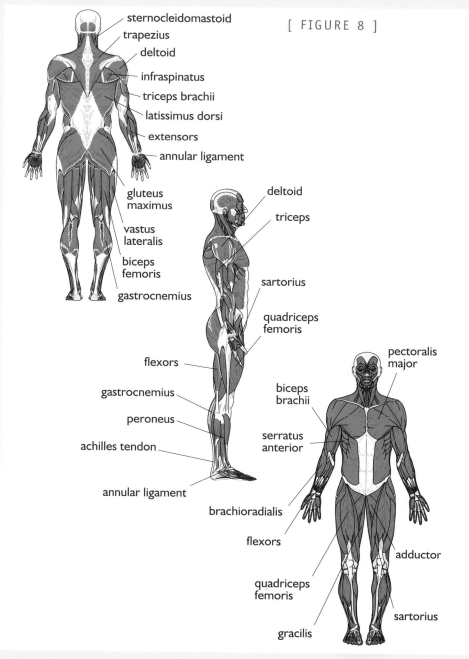

[FIGURE 8]

sternocleidomastoid
trapezius
deltoid
infraspinatus
triceps brachii
latissimus dorsi
extensors
annular ligament

gluteus maximus
vastus lateralis
biceps femoris
gastrocnemius

deltoid
triceps
sartorius
quadriceps femoris

flexors
gastrocnemius
peroneus
achilles tendon
annular ligament
brachioradialis
flexors
quadriceps femoris
gracilis

pectoralis major
biceps brachii
serratus anterior
adductor
sartorius

The major muscles of the body are shown from the back, side, and front.

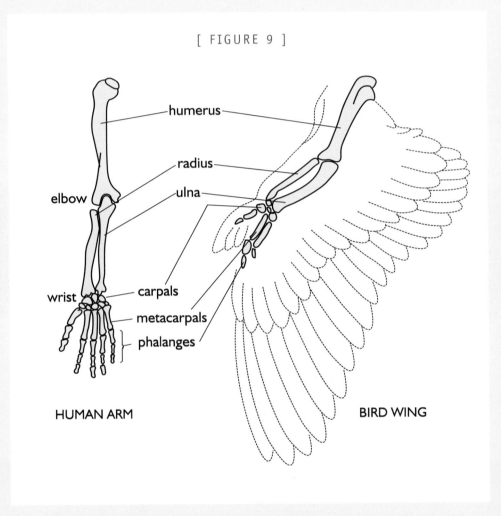

[FIGURE 9]

humerus

radius

ulna

elbow

wrist

carpals

metacarpals

phalanges

HUMAN ARM

BIRD WING

The bones of the human arm are very similar to the bones of a bird's wing.

Now that you have exposed the bones, find the wide, tough, white ligaments that connect the humerus to the radius and ulna. Cut away the ligaments with scissors in order to see the ends of the bones. Notice the shiny cartilage that covers the ends of the bones. How does the cartilage protect the bones? Do you find anything else within the joint (the space between the bones)?

When you have finished, save the bones for use in the next experiment and place all the other chicken wing tissues in the garbage. Then **wash your hands and utensils thoroughly with soap and water.**

 Science Fair Project Idea

One of the most serious athletic injuries involves tearing the anterior cruciate ligament in the knee. Investigate this injury and try to explain why it is so much more common among women than men.

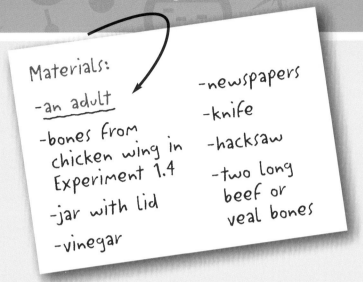

Materials:

-an adult

-bones from chicken wing in Experiment 1.4

-jar with lid

-vinegar

-newspapers

-knife

-hacksaw

-two long beef or veal bones

In Experiment 1.2 you learned that bones form a sound framework for your body. You located and identified many of the bones that make up your skeleton. But what about the internal structure of bones? What are bones made of and what else do they do? In this experiment, you will examine the internal structure of bones.

Place the dry humerus bone you saved from the previous experiment in a jar of vinegar. Does the bone sink or float? What does this tell you about the density of chicken bone? Do you think the bone of a seagull would be more or less dense than a chicken bone? What makes you think so?

Screw the lid on the jar and leave the other bones that you saved from Experiment 1.4 beside the jar. Vinegar is an acid. It will slowly dissolve the minerals in bone. These minerals constitute about two thirds of a bone's weight. Organic matter—bone and cartilage and blood vessel cells—make up the remaining third.

After several days, remove the bone from the jar. How does its flexibility compare with that of the dry bones you left beside the jar?

The soft, flexible, plasticlike material that remains after the minerals have been removed would eventually decay if buried in soil. Under proper conditions, the mineral or hard part of the whole bone would be preserved and form a fossil.

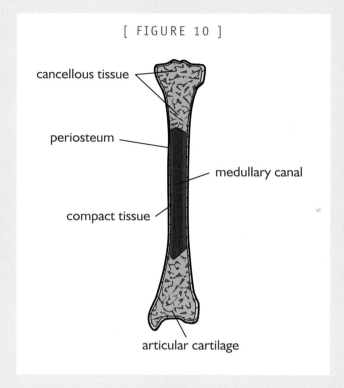

[FIGURE 10]

cancellous tissue

periosteum

medullary canal

compact tissue

articular cartilage

A longitudinal section of a human long bone.

Place the bone that you have soaked in vinegar on some newspapers. **Ask an adult** to use a knife to cut the bone in half along its long axis to make what is called a longitudinal section. Then you can see what lies inside the bone. It will resemble the drawing in Figure 10, which shows a longitudinal section of a human long bone. The dense, or compact, bony tissue along the outside of the bone makes up the shaft of long bones. The spongy, or cancellous, bony tissue is found inside the shaft and especially near the ends of a bone. The medullary canal runs along the central shaft of a long bone. It contains yellow marrow, which is mostly fatty tissue, and blood vessels. Red marrow, which is found near the ends of the long bones, contains cells known as erythroblasts.

Erythroblasts produce red blood cells, the cells in your blood that transport oxygen. Except for their cartilaginous ends, bones are covered by a membrane called periosteum. The widened end of a long bone is called the epiphysis. The wider ends give the joints greater stability and serve to reduce the pressure on the bones.

Having seen the longitudinal section of a chicken bone, try to predict what the cross section will look like. Then **ask the adult** to cut across one of the unsoftened bones with a hacksaw. Does the cross section look the way you thought it would?

If possible, obtain two long beef or veal bones from a butcher. He or she might even cut one of them longitudinally for you. You can **ask the adult** to make several cuts across the other one when you reach home.

How do the longitudinal and cross sections of the beef bones compare with those of the chicken bones? Does the medullary canal of the beef bone extend all the way into the epiphysis?

Science Fair Project Ideas

- Compare the densities of chicken and beef bones. Can you explain your results?
- What minerals are found in bones? What foods must you eat to supply the minerals needed to make bone?
- Paleontologists have found broken animal bones near the fossils of species believed to be the forerunners of today's humans. They believe the bones were broken to obtain the marrow that was inside. Why would these precursors of humans want bone marrow?

No Materials Needed

With more than six hundred skeletal muscles in your body, you can move your body in many ways. A skeletal muscle generally has its origin (attachment of one end) on one bone that remains relatively fixed. Its other end—its insertion—is attached to the bone that moves when the muscle contracts. Both attachments, whether origin or insertion, are made by fibrous tendons that connect muscle to bone.

In this experiment, you will feel and identify some of your muscles. You will find Figure 8 useful as you search for muscles. Perhaps the muscle most familiar to you is your biceps or, more properly, your biceps brachii. It is the muscle on your arm that you show when someone says, "Make a muscle." The *biceps* part of the name means that the muscle has two heads and two origins. The *brachii* part of the name is from the Latin word *bracchium*, which means "arm."

Both origins of the biceps brachii are on the shoulder. The insertion of this muscle is found at the upper end of the radius. Place your hand on your biceps as you make a muscle by contracting it. As the muscle shortens, two things happen. The radius is lifted (and with it the lower arm). At the same time, the radius is turned outward so that the palm of your hand is turned upward.

You can use another muscle—the brachialis—to bend your arm. The brachialis lies under the biceps. Its origin is on the humerus. Its insertion is on the ulna. Bend your arm again, but this time keep your palm turned downward so that the radius does not turn about the ulna. As you can feel, the biceps does not contract. It is pushed up a little by the contracting brachialis muscle, but the upper arm feels much more flaccid than it did before. Now turn the palm over. You will immediately feel the biceps pop up.

If a bone can be moved to a certain position, it can be returned to where it was previously. Muscles are paired so that movements can be reversed. Just as you can flex (bend) your arm by contracting your biceps or brachialis muscles, so you can use a muscle to extend (straighten) the arm. The muscle that straightens your arm is the triceps brachii. What can you tell about this muscle just from its name?

Place your hand on the back of your upper arm when your arm is flexed. Can you feel the triceps contract as you fully straighten your arm? What can you assume about the location of the triceps' insertion? Where might its origin(s) be located?

The large muscles that cover your shoulder joints and make them appear round are the deltoids (Figures 8 and 11). Their origins are on the clavicle, acromion process, and scapula. Their insertions are on the outside of the humerus bones. Can you predict what will happen when one of your deltoid muscles contracts? Try it. Were you right?

The pectoralis major opposes the action of the deltoid on the same side of the body. Place your hand on the upper side of your chest. You can feel pectoralis major contract as you pull your arm downward and move it across your chest. Explain how the origins and insertions of pectoralis major make this movement possible (see Figure 11).

The muscle that extends your fingers is the extensor digitorum communis (Figure 12a). It can be felt the on the upper side of your lower arm when you extend your fingers. At the same time, beneath the skin on the back of your hand you can see the movement of the tendons that connect the muscle to the fingers. Extending your index finger alone will enable you to see a single tendon moving beneath the skin.

Figure 12b shows the flexor digitorum profundus, which you use to bend your fingers. Place your fingers on the inside of your opposite forearm and feel this muscle contract. At the same time, you can see the tendons that connect this muscle to the fingers moving beneath the skin on your forearm. Can you find the muscles that extend and flex your thumbs? Can you see the movement of the tendons that connect these muscles to the thumbs?

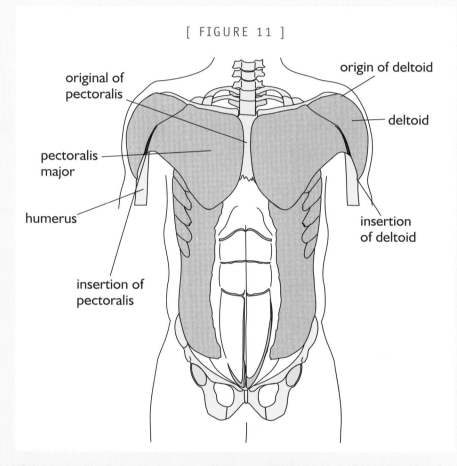

[FIGURE 11]

original of
pectoralis

origin of deltoid

deltoid

pectoralis
major

humerus

insertion
of deltoid

insertion of
pectoralis

These muscles have opposite effects on the motion of the humerus.
The deltoids (there is also one in the rear that has its origin on the
scapula) lift the humerus. The pectoralis lowers the humerus.

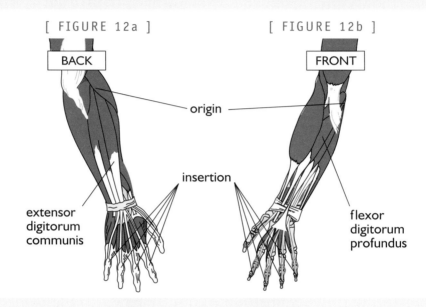

[FIGURE 12a]

BACK

origin

insertion

extensor
digitorum
communis

[FIGURE 12b]

FRONT

flexor
digitorum
profundus

Opposing muscles extend (a) and flex (b) the fingers of the right hand.

 Science Fair Project Ideas

- Find the muscles and tendons used to flex and extend your knee joint. Then find the muscles used to flex and extend your foot. Use an anatomy book to find the names as well as the origins and insertions of these muscles.
- What is the advantage of having the muscles that control the fingers and thumbs located so far from the hands?
- The gastrocnemius and soleus muscles in your calf are connected to your heel bone by the Achilles tendon. It is the strongest and thickest tendon in your body. You can find the story of Achilles in a book on Greek mythology. After reading the story, explain why this tendon was named for him.

Chapter 2

The Circulatory, Respiratory, and Digestive Systems

THE PROCESS OF RESPIRATION PROVIDES CELLS WITH THE ENERGY THEY NEED TO LIVE. The energy comes from the reaction between oxygen (obtained through respiration) and food. The reaction provides energy and releases carbon dioxide and water as waste products. In single-celled animals the oxygen and food simply diffuse across a cell membrane. The waste products leave the cell in the same way.

Humans have trillions of cells. Most of them are surrounded by other cells. The cells depend on blood to bring the food and oxygen they need and to carry away the waste products they produce. Blood circulates throughout the body inside blood vessels that lead to and from the heart. Arteries carry oxygen-rich blood from the heart, and veins carry the depleted blood back to the heart and then to the lungs. Between arteries and veins are capillaries—vessels with walls that are only one cell thick. It is through the walls of these tiny vessels that molecules of oxygen and food diffuse from the blood to the body cells. Similarly, waste products from the cells, such as carbon dioxide, diffuse into the blood through these same walls.

In your lungs, oxygen in the air you breathe diffuses into the blood. Carbon dioxide in your blood diffuses out into air that is exhaled from your lungs through your mouth and nose. The blood, which carries these gases to and from your lungs, is pumped to the lungs and to all the cells of your body by your heart.

YOU HAVE A HEART

Despite its association with such emotions and virtues as love and courage, the heart is basically a four-chambered pump. Figure 13a shows how the blood pumped from the heart circulates around the body. The blood vessels that contain blood rich in oxygen are shaded. Those that contain blood from which much of the oxygen has been removed are unshaded. The direction of blood flow is shown by the small arrows. A more detailed drawing of the heart itself is shown in Figure 13b.

Deoxygenated blood (blood that has lost much of its oxygen) is carried by several large veins to the heart's right atrium. The heart's contraction begins in the atria and forces blood into the ventricles. As contraction continues, deoxygenated blood in the right ventricle is pumped out of the heart into the pulmonary artery. This artery, which divides into right and left branches, transports blood to the lungs. These arteries divide further and eventually become capillaries, where the blood picks up oxygen from air inside the lungs. At the same time, it releases carbon dioxide to air in the lungs.

After being oxygenated, the blood enters the pulmonary veins and is carried to the heart's left atrium. Blood in this atrium is pumped into the left ventricle and from there out of the heart into the aorta—the body's major artery. The aorta divides into smaller arteries that bring blood to cells throughout the body. After giving up much of its oxygen in capillaries, blood returns to the heart's right atrium through veins.

The entire heart does not contract at the same time. A natural pacemaker, controlled by the vagus nerve from the brain, is located in the right atrium. It generates an electrical impulse that causes the heart to contract. The contraction begins in the atria, forcing blood in the atria through the bicuspid, or mitral valve, and tricuspid valve into the ventricles. When the impulse reaches the ventricles, they too contact.

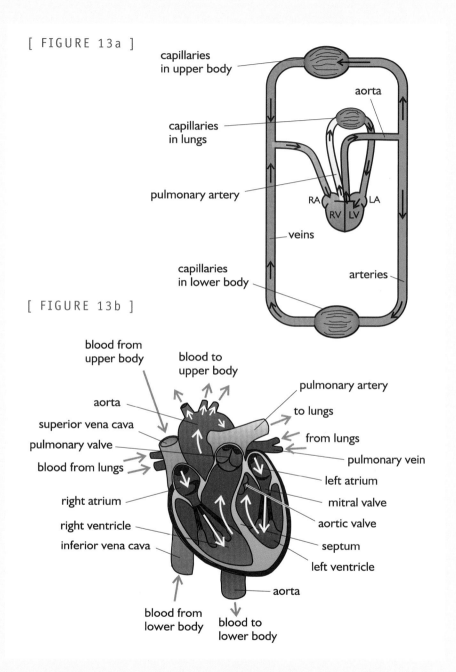

capillaries
in upper body

aorta

capillaries
in lungs

pulmonary artery

RA   LA

RV   LV

veins

capillaries
in lower body

arteries

blood from
upper body

blood to
upper body

pulmonary artery

aorta

to lungs

superior vena cava

from lungs

pulmonary valve

pulmonary vein

blood from lungs

left atrium

right atrium

mitral valve

aortic valve

right ventricle

septum

inferior vena cava

left ventricle

aorta

blood from
lower body

blood to
lower body

13a) The general nature of the circulatory system. (R = right; L = left; A = atrium; V = ventricle) b) This is a more detailed look at the heart and the vessels leading to it (veins) and from it (arteries).

Their contraction slams shut the valves between the atria and ventricles and pushes blood out through the aortic and pulmonary valves into the aorta and pulmonary artery. After contracting, the heart relaxes and blood begins to pour into the atria from the body's major veins. At the same time, the blood pressure in the ventricles becomes less than in the aorta and pulmonary artery. This causes the aortic and pulmonary valves to close.

2.1 Listening to a Heart

Materials:
- stethoscope or a friend
- stopwatch, or clock or watch with second hand
- rubber ball

If you have access to a stethoscope, you can listen to your own heart. Place the ear tips in your ears and the chest piece slightly to the left of the center of your chest. Move the chest piece slightly until you hear the heart sounds most clearly. Listen for two sounds in close succession. The first is a relatively long booming sound. The second is a short, sharp sound. Together they sound like "lubb-dup." The *lubb* is caused by the contracting muscle and the closing of the valves between the ventricles and atria. The *dup* is the sound of the aortic and pulmonary valves closing.

If you do not have a stethoscope, you can hear the same sounds by placing your ear against the chest of a friend. Your friend will probably want to hear your heart as well.

You have heard the heart of a body at rest. Do you think there will be any change in the sounds after exercise?

To find out, run in place for five minutes. Or have your friend run in place for the same length of time. Then listen to your heart or his. Are the sounds the same or different? If they are different, can you explain why they are different?

To have some understanding of how much work your heart does, hold a rubber ball in your hand. The ball represents the blood that must be squeezed out of the heart with each beat. Your hand represents the heart muscle that will do the squeezing. Squeeze the ball at a steady rate of once every second.

How does your hand feel after several minutes? For your heart to consistently pump blood every minute of your life, it needs energy. That energy comes from the food carried to the muscle cells of your heart by the blood. Why is it essential that the blood flow to your heart not be obstructed or blocked?

 Science Fair Project Ideas

- What is an electrocardiograph and what is it used for? Examine an electrocardiogram. What is the significance of each part of the pattern? How does a cardiologist use an electrocardiogram to look for defects in a patient's heart?
- What is lymph? What is the lymphatic system? What functions does it serve? What causes lymphatic fluid to move? From where and to where does it move?

2.2 Finding a Pulse

Materials:

-a friend

-stethoscope

-table

-clay

-straw

With each contraction, your heart forces blood out into the arteries. The added blood swells the elastic walls of the large arteries near the heart, sending a pulse of expansion along the walls of all the arteries. You can feel this expansion of the radial artery in your wrist. Just place the first two fingers of one hand on the inside of your other wrist right behind your thumb, as shown in Figure 14a. Does each throb of your pulse reveal a beat of your heart?

To find out, place a stethoscope on a friend's chest and listen to his heart. While listening to his heart, place one hand on his pulse. Does the pulse follow closely after the heartbeat? What do your results tell you?

You can amplify the pulse in your wrist so that the pulse wave that travels along the radial artery can be seen. Place your forearm on a

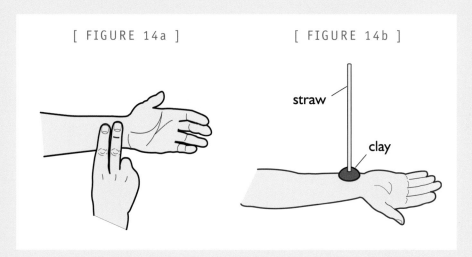

[FIGURE 14a]   [FIGURE 14b]

straw

clay

14a) A pulse can be felt on the inside of your wrist just behind your thumb. b) You can use a lump of clay and a drinking straw to amplify your pulse and make it visible.

table, palm side up. Put a small lump of clay on the skin that lies directly over the point where you feel your strongest pulse. Stick a straw in the clay as shown in Figure 14b. Watch the top of the straw. You will see it move with each beat of your heart.

You can find a pulse on any artery that is close to the surface of the body. For example, you can feel the pulsing of the carotid arteries in your neck on either side of your Adam's apple (larynx). With a stethoscope, you can listen to the blood flowing through your carotid arteries. Describe the sound.

You can also feel (and sometimes see) the pulse of the temporal artery just in front of your ear. In what other places on your body can you find a pulse? If you find a pulse at a point on the left side of your body, can you always find a pulse on the corresponding point on the right side?

Place the fingers of one hand on a friend's wrist pulse. Place the fingers of your other hand on the pulse in front of your friend's ear. Do you expect to feel both pulses at the same time or to feel one pulse before the other? What do you find? How can you explain the results of this experiment?

If you take your friend's pulse at both his neck and his wrist, which pulse do you expect to feel first? Try it. Were you right?

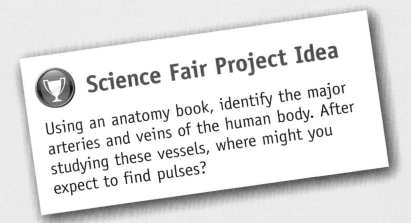

Science Fair Project Idea

Using an anatomy book, identify the major arteries and veins of the human body. After studying these vessels, where might you expect to find pulses?

Materials:
- cloth tape measure
- a friend
- pen or pencil
- notebook

Place a cloth tape measure around a friend's chest at armpit level. What happens to the circumference of his chest when he takes a deep breath? What happens to the circumference of his chest when he expires as much air as possible?

Now place the tape measure around his abdomen at belly button (navel) level. What happens to the circumference of his abdomen when he takes a deep breath? What happens to it after he expires as much air as possible?

Design a means of measuring the front-to-back thickness of your friend's chest and abdomen following a deep inhalation and a forceful expiration.

As you have seen, your abdomen and chest both grow in circumference when you inhale. Your diaphragm, which separates your chest and abdominal cavities, contracts, pushing your stomach and other organs in your abdomen downward. At the same time, the intercostal muscles in your chest lift your ribs upward and outward. The result of these movements increases the size of your chest and lungs. The increased volume reduces the air pressure in your lungs, which causes the air pressure outside your body to be greater than the pressure inside. As a result, air is forced into your lungs. This inhaled air travels along the trachea and bronchi (bronchial tubes), which branch into smaller and smaller tubes that finally end in tiny air sacs called alveoli (see Figure 15). The alveoli are surrounded by capillaries. It is through these capillaries that oxygen enters the blood. It is there, too, that carbon dioxide passes from blood to air in the alveoli.

When you exhale, just the opposite happens. The rib cage falls, the diaphragm rises, and the air pressure in your lungs increases until it

[FIGURE 15]

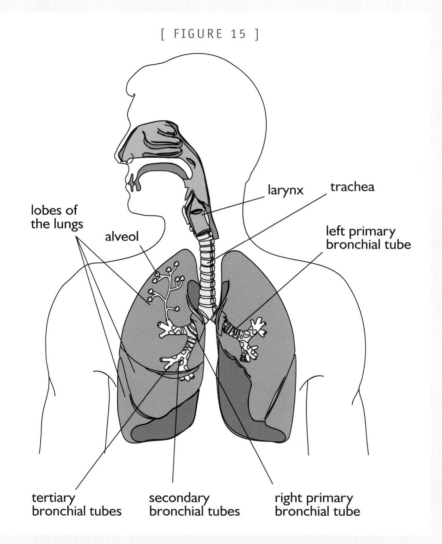

Air passes from your mouth or nose to your trachea, bronchial tubes, and eventually to the alveoli, where gases (oxygen and carbon dioxide) are exchanged between blood and air.

exceeds the air pressure outside. Then air is forced out of your lungs: You exhale.

Often when you have a cold, your nose is filled with mucus. Fortunately, you are still able to breathe. Hold your nose. Can you still breathe? How does the air reach your lungs? Now close your mouth. How does the air reach your lungs? What must be true about your mouth and nose?

 Science Fair Project Idea

What causes hiccups? How are they related to breathing? There are lots of "cures" for hiccups. Do any of them work?

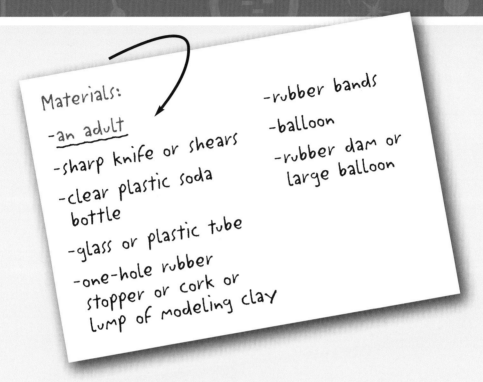

Materials:

-an adult
-sharp knife or shears
-clear plastic soda
  bottle
-glass or plastic tube
-one-hole rubber
  stopper or cork or
  lump of modeling clay
-rubber bands
-balloon
-rubber dam or
  large balloon

You can make a model to show how we breathe. **Ask an adult** to help you cut off the bottom of a clear plastic soda bottle. **Ask the same adult** to insert a glass or plastic tube through a one-hole rubber stopper, cork, or lump of modeling clay. Use a rubber band to fasten the neck of a balloon to the lower end of the tube. The balloon represents a lung. Insert the stopper, cork, or clay into the mouth of the bottle as shown in Figure 16. The tube represents the trachea that connects your lungs with your mouth.

To represent the diaphragm, fasten a rubber dam or the lower two thirds of a large balloon to the bottom of the bottle using long, strong rubber bands.

What happens to the balloon (lung) inside the bottle (chest cavity) when you pull down on the diaphragm? Why does it happen? What happens when you release the diaphragm? Why does it happen?

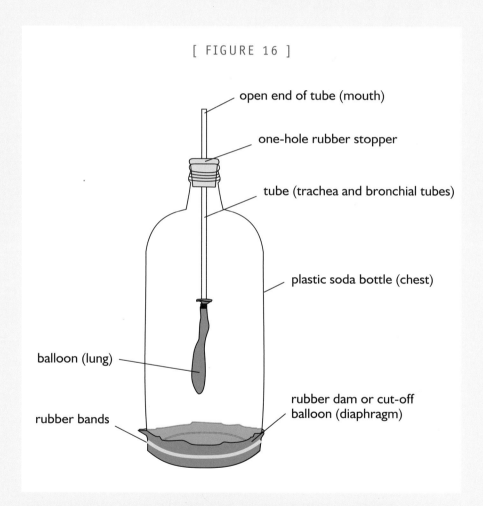

[FIGURE 16]

open end of tube (mouth)

one-hole rubber stopper

tube (trachea and bronchial tubes)

plastic soda bottle (chest)

balloon (lung)

rubber dam or cut-off
balloon (diaphragm)

rubber bands

You can make a model that shows how we breathe. The words in the parentheses show what various pieces of the model represent.

WHAT HAPPENS TO THE FOOD WE EAT?

Most of the energy stored in food would be of no value were it not digested. Molecules of protein, fat, starch, and disaccharides are too large to pass through the membranes of the cells that line the walls of the intestines. However, enzymes produced by the salivary glands, stomach, small intestine, and pancreas break these large molecules into smaller ones that can pass through cell membranes. These smaller molecules, such as glucose, fructose, fatty acids, and amino acids, enter the bloodstream and eventually reach all the cells of our bodies.

Like gasoline in a car, food in the body is "burned" to release energy. In your body, food is "burned" in a series of steps, each releasing some energy for the body's use. For example, energy released by one of these reactions might be used to make a muscle cell contract. Like the compression or stretching of a spring, the contraction of a muscle cell requires energy.

The waste products of these chemical reactions that release energy as they take place in the body's cells are carbon dioxide and water. These waste products are excreted from the body by the lungs and

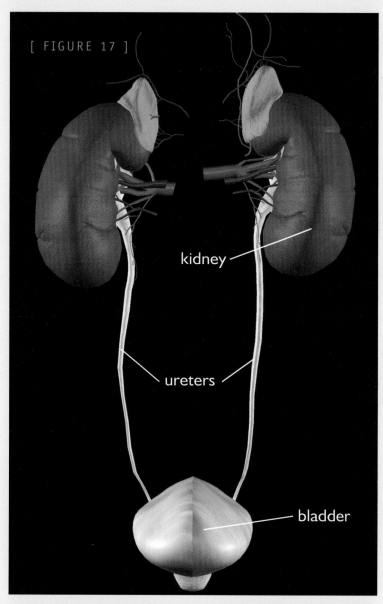

[FIGURE 17]

kidney

ureters

bladder

Urine is produced in the kidneys, which filter waste from the blood. The urine flows through ureters to the bladder, where it collects. The bladder is emptied periodically.

kidneys. In the lungs, the wastes are expelled as gases when we exhale. In the kidneys, wastes, such as urea, bicarbonates, excess salts, vitamins, and water, are filtered from the blood and carried to the bladder through the ureters, a pair of tubes that connect the kidneys with the bladder (Figure 17). Urea is produced from the breakdown of protein, and bicarbonates are formed from the reaction of carbon dioxide with water in the blood. When the bladder becomes full, the fluid waste, urine, is excreted through the urethra. The kidneys and bladder make up yet another body system—the excretory system.

The next two experiments will allow you to see how some food is digested. You will observe the action of digestive enzymes and learn about how food is broken down so it can be absorbed and used by cells.

Materials:

- an adult
- medicine cups or vials
- eyedropper
- lemon juice
- cornstarch
- water
- cooking pan
- stove
- sugarless gum
- small test tubes or vials
- tincture of iodine
- alcohol thermometer
- container to hold warm water
- pen or pencil
- notebook
- soda cracker
- plastic wrap

As you may know, starch is a carbohydrate that can be identified by the addition of iodine, which causes the formation of a dark blue color. The digestion of starch begins in the mouth, where it is acted on by amylase, an enzyme found in saliva. Saliva is secreted by salivary glands found in your cheeks.

To see the action of the amylase, you will need to collect some saliva. To begin, simply let saliva collect in your mouth for a period of five minutes. Then spit the liquid into a medicine cup. How much saliva accumulated in your mouth during the five-minute period?

Next, use a clean eyedropper to place a few drops of lemon juice on your tongue. Again, measure the volume of saliva that collects during the next five minutes. How do the two volumes you collected compare? How do your salivary glands respond to the presence of food in your mouth?

To test the effect of amylase on starch, you will need to prepare a starch mixture. Do this by mixing one gram of cornstarch (about one teaspoonful) with 100 ml of water. Pour the mixture into a small cooking pan and, **under adult supervision**, bring the mixture to a boil on a stove.

While the liquid is heating, chew some sugarless gum. How will this help to provide an abundant supply of saliva? Spit the saliva you generate into a medicine cup. This is the saliva you will use to react with the starch.

Once the starch-water mixture is boiling, remove it from the stove and let it cool. Use an eyedropper to remove about 2 ml of the cooled starchy liquid and place it in a small test tube or vial. Place another 2 ml in an identical vessel. Then add about the same amount of saliva and a drop of tincture of iodine to the liquid in the first test tube. To the second test tube, add 2 ml of water and a drop of tincture of iodine. What color changes do you observe? What causes the color changes? Record your results in your notebook.

Be sure you can distinguish the test tube that contains saliva from the one that contains water. Then place both tubes in a water bath at body temperature (37°C or 98.6°F). What is the purpose of the tube with water, starch, and iodine?

Watch the two tubes over the next hour or two. What changes in color do you observe? What can you conclude about the effect of saliva on starch? Record your results.

Another way to see the action of amylase is to look at its effect on the starch in food. To see this effect, chew a soda cracker for five minutes so that it becomes thoroughly mixed with your saliva. Spit the chewed cracker and saliva into a medicine cup.

With an eyedropper, remove a small amount of the chewed cracker and place it in another medicine cup. Then add a drop of tincture of iodine. What can you conclude? Has all the starch been digested? Record your results.

Cover the cup that contains the chewed cracker and saliva with a piece of plastic wrap. After several hours, test another sample of the chewed cracker and saliva with iodine. Continue to test for starch at intervals of about six hours for several days.

Is the starch eventually digested? If it is, how long did it take?

Although the digestion of starch begins in the mouth, it is completed in the intestine where amylase secreted by the pancreas changes starch to disaccharide sugars. The disaccharides, in turn, are broken into monosaccharide sugars by enzymes secreted from the glands in the wall of the small intestine. What evidence do you have from your experiments that would suggest the digestion of starch is not completed in the mouth?

 Science Fair Project Ideas

- Design and carry out an experiment to determine whether the amylase in saliva can digest starch all the way to a monosaccharide sugar, such as glucose. What do you conclude?
- Can you swallow food or drink through a straw when your head is lower than your stomach? If you can, how is the food moved upward from your mouth to your stomach?

Materials:

- an adult

- hard-boiled egg

- safety glasses

- knife

- 4 test tubes or glass vials

- balance

- pepsin (available from school or science supply company)

- masking tape or labels

- dilute (1.0 molar) hydrochloric acid (probably available from school science department)

- incubator or small oven that will allow you to keep temperature at 37°C (98°F)

- graduated cylinder or metric measuring cup

- olive oil

- pancreatic lipase (available from school or science supply company)

- water

PEPSIN

One of the enzymes found in your stomach is pepsin. Your stomach also secretes hydrochloric acid. Pepsin in an acidic environment will break proteins into shorter chains of amino acids called peptides. Later, in the intestine, another enzyme (trypsin) will break the peptides into individual amino acids.

To see the action of pepsin on a protein, **ask an adult** to help you make a hard-boiled egg. **Put on safety glasses.** Place two small pieces of egg white from the hard-boiled egg into each of two test tubes or glass vials. To one tube or vial add 0.5 g of pepsin powder. Label this tube "P-enzyme." **Ask an adult** to pour 10 ml of dilute (1.0 molar) hydrochloric acid into both tubes or vials. Place both tubes in an incubator or small oven that will allow you to keep the tubes at about 37°C (98°F) for the next forty-eight hours. Examine both tubes at twelve-hour intervals. What changes do you observe? How does the egg white in the tube with the enzyme and acid differ from the tube that contains only acid?

LIPASE

Lipase is an enzyme secreted into the small intestine by the pancreas. It breaks fats and oils into fatty acids and glycerine. To see the action of lipase, add 2 ml of olive oil to each of two test tubes or glass vials. To one tube or vial add 10 ml of a saturated solution of pancreatic lipase. Label this tube "L-enzyme." Pour 10 ml of water into the other tube or vial. Place both tubes in an incubator or small oven that will allow you to keep the tubes at about 37°C (98°F) for the next forty-eight hours. Examine both tubes at twelve-hour intervals. What changes do you observe? How does the oil in the tube with the lipase differ from the tube that contains only water?

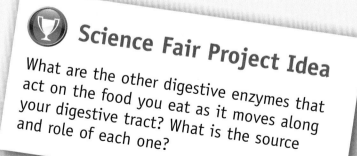

Science Fair Project Idea

What are the other digestive enzymes that act on the food you eat as it moves along your digestive tract? What is the source and role of each one?

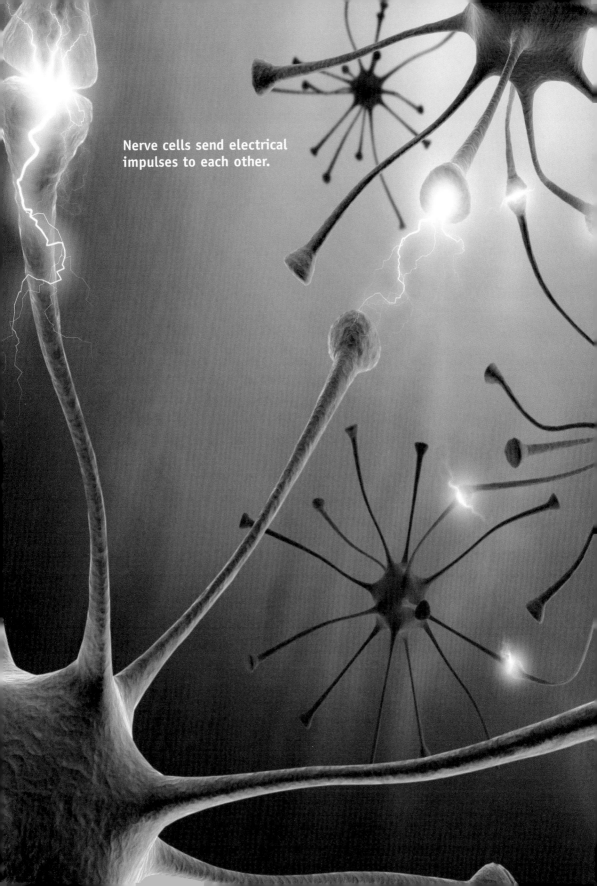

Nerve cells send electrical
impulses to each other.

Chapter 3

The Nervous and Endocrine Systems

THERE ARE TWO BODY SYSTEMS THAT CONTROL AND COORDINATE YOUR BODY. They are the nervous system and the endocrine system.

The hypothalamus, located at the base of the brain, links the nervous and endocrine systems. The hypothalamus releases chemicals that affect the pituitary gland, which lies beneath the hypothalamus. The pituitary, in turn, controls many other glands by its release of hormones that stimulate other endocrine glands. For that reason, the pituitary has often been called the master gland.

THE NERVOUS SYSTEM

Your nervous system controls and coordinates actions that take place in your body. The central nervous system, which consists of the brain and spinal cord, is well protected. The brain is enclosed within the skull, and the spinal cord lies inside the vertebrae that make up the backbone. The nerves that emerge from the central nervous system and connect it with the rest of the body constitute the peripheral nervous system.

Nerve cells (neurons), shown in Figure 18a, respond to stimuli both inside and outside the body. A stimulus causes electrical action—an impulse—that travels in one direction along the nerve cell from dendrite

[FIGURE 18a]

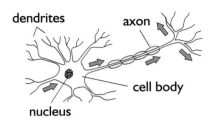

dendrites
axon
cell body
nucleus

[FIGURE 18b]

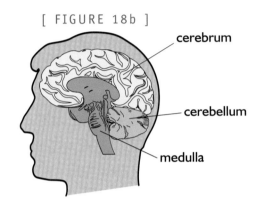

cerebrum
cerebellum
medulla

[FIGURE 18c]

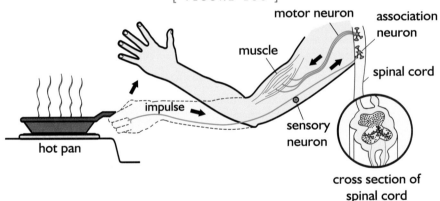

motor neuron
association neuron
muscle
spinal cord
impulse
sensory neuron
hot pan
cross section of spinal cord

18a) A nerve impulse moves along a nerve cell (neuron). The impulse starts in a dendrite. It travels to the cell body and then along an axon to another neuron or muscle. b) The three main parts of the brain are the cerebrum, cerebellum, and medulla (or brain stem). c) Reflexes such as this one can protect you from harm. You touch something hot and immediately pull your hand away. The reflex allows you to react without thinking.

to cell body to axon. Neurons are not connected to one another. There is a gap between the axon of one nerve cell and the dendrites of another. The gap is called a synapse. Chemicals produced at the end of a nerve cell's axon carry an impulse across the synapse to the dendrites of another neuron.

There are three types of neurons: sensory, association, and motor. Sensory neurons carry impulses from sense organs, such as your eyes, ears, nose, and the sensory receptors in your skin and internal organs, to your central nervous system. Association neurons connect sensory and motor neurons. Motor neurons transmit nerve impulses to muscles.

Most impulses that travel along motor neurons arise in the brain. For example, you see a ball that is thrown to you by means of sensory impulses that travel from your eyes to the back of your brain. Association neurons carry these impulses to motor neurons that cause the muscles in your arms to move your hands so that they can catch the ball.

The region of the brain that coordinates the impulses that allow you to catch a ball is the cerebrum (Figure 18b). It is the largest part of the human brain. It is the part concerned with memories, thoughts, learning, speech, and voluntary movements. At the rear of the brain and under the cerebrum is the cerebellum. It coordinates nerve impulses to and from the cerebrum and also controls muscle coordination, including those that keep your body balanced. The medulla, which lies at the base of the brain, controls impulses that regulate such involuntary actions as breathing, heartbeat, and contractions of smooth muscles.

Not all motor impulses arise in the brain. Some are reflex actions—automatic responses to stimuli that arise in a sensory organ. The impulse passes along a sensory neuron to an association neuron in the spinal cord, and from there to a motor neuron that carries an impulse to a muscle or muscles. You may be aware of a reflex action, but it is automatic. It happens before you have time to think about it. Figure 18c shows a reflex reaction that occurs when you touch something hot.

Normal body functions are maintained or adjusted to meet immediate needs by the autonomic nervous system. Impulses in the autonomic system are below the level of consciousness. Nerve cells that are part of the autonomic system arise in the medulla or spinal cord. There are two divisions to this system, the sympathetic and parasympathetic. The effects of the two divisions generally produce opposite effects on the smooth muscles, heart muscle, and glands that they control. In general, the sympathetic nervous system prepares the body for action in response to stress. The parasympathetic system produces opposite effects and keeps the body in a more relaxed state. Effects of the two systems are summarized in Table 1.

TABLE 1
Effects of sympathetic and parasympathetic divisions of the autonomic nervous system

Sympathetic	Parasympathetic
Dilates pupils of the eyes	Contracts pupils of the eyes
Dilates bronchial tubes	Constricts bronchial tubes
Increases heart rate	Decreases heart rate
Increases strength of heart contractions	Decreases strength of heart contractions
Intestinal movements reduced	Intestinal movements increased
Increases secretions of glands	Decreases secretions of glands

THE ENDOCRINE SYSTEM

The endocrine system (Figure 19) is made up of glands that secrete chemical substances known as hormones into the blood. Hormones are chemical "messengers" that cause changes in certain parts of the body. Table 2 provides information about the major endocrine glands.

[FIGURE 19]

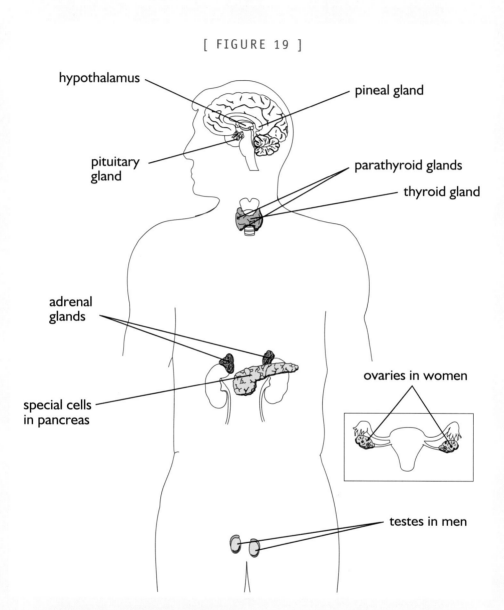

hypothalamus

pineal gland

pituitary
gland

parathyroid glands

thyroid gland

adrenal
glands

ovaries in women

special cells
in pancreas

testes in men

The major organs that make up the body's endocrine system

TABLE 2

The major endocrine glands, the hormones they produce, and the hormones' effects on the body

Gland	Hormone(s) Produced	Effect of Hormone
pituitary	GH (growth hormone)	controls growth of body
	gonadotropic hormone	stimulates hormone production in ovaries or testes
	TSH (thyroid-stimulating hormone)	influences thyroid gland
	ACTH (adrenocorticotropic hormone)	influences cortex of adrenal gland
	FSH (follicle-stimulating hormone)	causes eggs to develop in ovary; maintains seminiferous tubules in testes
	LH (luteinizing hormone)	influences ovaries and testes
	ADH (antidiuretic hormone)	controls body's water and salt balance
	oxytocin	stimulates milk production and contractions of the uterus
pineal	melatonin	controls body rhythms such as sleeping
thyroid	thyroxin	controls body's metabolism
	thyrocalcitonin	lowers blood calcium and phosphate
parathyroid	parathyroid hormone	increases blood calcium and phosphate
adrenal: cortex—	mineralcorticoids	regulates salt and water balance in body
	cortisone	regulates metabolism of food
medulla—	adrenaline (epinephrine)	controls body's response to stress by stimulating carbohydrate metabolism
	noradrenaline (norepinephrine)	controls body's response to stress by increasing heart rate and blood pressure
kidney	erythropoietin	stimulates production of red blood cells
	renin	increases blood flow
pancreas	insulin	reduces blood sugar level
	glucagon	raises blood sugar level
ovary	estrogen	stimulates development of secondary sexual characteristics
	progesterone	prepares uterus for pregnancy
testes	testosterone	causes development of secondary sexual characteristics

Materials:

- pencil
- large one-hole rubber stopper
- a friend
- table
- stopwatch, or clock or watch with second hand
- flashlight
- chair
- sheet of cardboard

There are many reflex actions that take place in your body. Doctors sometimes test a patient to see if any of the common reflexes are missing. The reason for doing this is that the association neurons responsible for different reflexes are located at different levels in the spinal cord. By determining which reflexes are not working, a doctor can determine the site of nerve damage.

Reflexes that involve the autonomic nervous system are involuntary. You cannot control them by willful muscle action. Reflexes that reach the conscious level of the brain may be controlled by voluntary action, at least to some extent.

With a friend to serve as a subject, you can examine a number of human reflexes. You can also check to see which ones are controlled by the autonomic nervous system.

PATELLAR REFLEX

The reflex with which you are probably most familiar is the knee jerk. It is the one your doctor checks when you have a physical examination.

He or she probably uses a rubber hammer to hit your lower leg just below the kneecap. You can make your own rubber hammer by inserting a pencil into a large one-hole rubber stopper.

To test this reflex yourself, have a friend sit on a table with her lower leg relaxed and hanging from the edge of the table. Use your rubber hammer to strike your friend's leg just below the kneecap and just above the top of the tibia. This stretches the patellar tendon and should elicit the reflex. The response is the contraction of the quadriceps muscle, which pulls the lower leg upward (see Figure 20). Can your friend willfully prevent the reflex from happening by tightening her leg muscles?

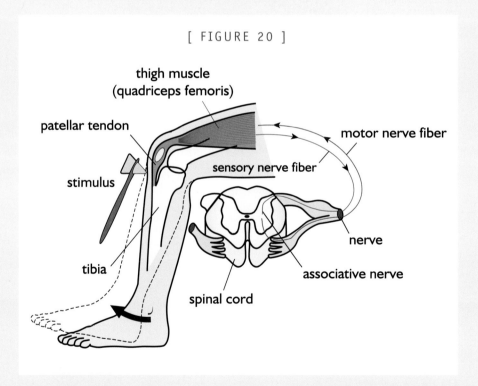

[FIGURE 20]

The patellar reflex: Stretching the patellar tendon by tapping it is the stimulus for a reflex that causes the thigh muscle to contract, thus raising the lower leg.

How does the time for the patellar reflex stimulus to work compare with the voluntary response to a verbal command to kick your leg upward? How can you explain any difference in the time between stimulus and response for these two actions?

PUPILLARY REFLEX

Examine the pupils of your subject's eyes in normal light. Then have her close her eyes for at least one minute. When she opens her eyes, what do you notice about the size of her pupils? What happens to their size once they are in brighter light?

Use a flashlight to shine a light into one eye of your subject. What happens to the size of the pupil in that eye? Does the pupil of the other eye respond in the same way? Can your subject willfully prevent her pupils from responding to changes in light intensity?

CILIOSPINAL REFLEX

Watch a subject's pupils as you gently move the hairs on the back of her neck. What happens to the size of the pupils? What happens to the subject's pupils if you pinch the back of her neck?

BLINKING REFLEX

Ask someone to sit quietly in a chair. Without warning, **but with care not to touch the eyes**, wave your hand in front of his face. What happens? Can he willfully control this reflex and not blink?

Have your subject hold a sheet of cardboard about as long as his head perpendicular to the center of his face. The purpose of the cardboard (which should not be known to the subject) is to prevent the air you blow into one eye from reaching the other eye.

With cardboard barrier in place, blow into one eye. Does the eye you blow into blink? Does the other eye blink, too? Can the subject willfully control this reflex and not blink when you blow into one of his eyes?

Science Fair Project Ideas

- Test the reflexes you have examined on a number of different people. Do some respond faster than others? Do the responses vary in any way? Does age or gender seem to affect an individual's reflexes?
- Can you find other reflexes that are common to all humans?
- With the permission of its parent, test the reflexes of a baby that is just a few days old. What happens when you touch the baby's cheek near its mouth? What happens when you place your index finger across the baby's palm? Do these reflexes have any survival value?
- What are the Moro and walking reflexes found in babies? Ask the parent of a baby if he or she has seen these reflexes.

Materials:

- a friend
- shower
- alcohol thermometer to measure air temperature
- alcohol or digital thermometer to measure body temperature
- stopwatch, or clock or watch with second hand
- pen or pencil
- notebook
- lab thermometer
- device to measure blood pressure
- bucket or sink
- ice water

The hypothalamus is your body's thermostat. It responds to the temperature of blood by sending impulses to blood vessels in the skin. The impulses direct these vessels to dilate or contract. By dilating, they bring more warm blood close to the body's surface and thereby cool the body by increasing heat loss through the skin. By contracting, they reduce heat loss. How do you think impulses from the hypothalamus might affect the heart as a means of responding to body temperature?

To see how your hypothalamus controls body temperature, you can take a hot shower and record your body temperature, heart rate, and air temperature at different times during the shower. You can then continue to take data on your temperature and heart rate as you cool off after the shower.

Prepare a data table similar to Table 3. Ask a friend outside the shower to watch the time and record data in the table you have prepared.

TABLE 3

Data table to see how body temperature and heart rate respond to changes in temperature

Time (min)	Body Temp.	Heart Rate (beats/min)	Room Temp.	Air Temp. in Shower	Water Temp.
Before Shower					
During Shower 2					
5					
10					
After Shower 2					
4					
6					

DO NOT WRITE IN THIS BOOK!

Before entering the shower, place a thermometer that can measure air temperature in the bathroom. Place a digital or alcohol thermometer under your tongue for two minutes. During the second minute, take your pulse to obtain your heart rate. After two minutes remove and read the thermometer, and have your friend record your temperature, heart rate, and room temperature in the data table.

To avoid slippery hands, which could cause you to drop the thermometer, **do not use soap while taking this shower.**

Place the thermometer in your mouth and observe your skin color as you enter the hot shower. **Be sure to keep the mouth thermometer away from the hot water!** Keep the shower water as hot as possible without feeling uncomfortable. Your partner will let you know when one minute has passed. At that point begin counting your heart beats by taking your pulse. Your partner will again let you know when two minutes have passed. At that time, remove the thermometer and report your heart rate and your body temperature to your partner. Your partner can record that data as well as room temperature.

Your partner will inform you when 4, 5, 9, and 10 minutes have passed so that body temperature, heart rate, and room temperature can be recorded at 5 and 10 minutes after you enter the shower. Between 5 and 7 minutes, if possible, ask your partner to hand you a lab thermometer so that you can measure the temperature of the water in the shower.

After ten minutes, turn off the shower and open the bathroom window or door so that the air around you cools. Observe your skin color and record heart rate, body temperature, and room temperature at 2, 4, and 6 minutes after coming out of the shower.

Compare the changes in room temperature with changes in body temperature. Compare body temperatures with the hot water's temperature.

How did your skin color before and immediately after the shower compare? What can you conclude?

To see how the hypothalamus responds to a falling temperature, have a subject sit quietly in a room at a comfortable temperature when it is very cool or cold outside. Record the subject's body temperature, heart rate (pulse), and blood pressure. Also note her skin color and temperature (warm, cool, or cold). Then turn down the thermostat and open windows to make the room as cool as possible. After a few minutes, again record the subject's body temperature, heart rate, blood pressure, and note her skin color and temperature.

Based on the data you have collected, what signals does the hypothalamus send to the heart and blood vessels of the skin when there is sudden drop in the temperature of the environment?

Instead of placing a subject's entire body in a cold environment, fill a bucket or sink with ice water and have your subject place her hand in it for one minute. Record the subject's body temperature, heart rate, and blood pressure before and at one-minute intervals after she removes her hand from the ice water. Also note her skin color and temperature. Does the body respond differently if only a small part of the body rather than the entire body is exposed to a cold temperature?

PERCEPTION

At this moment you are being bombarded by stimuli—light from all the objects around you; sounds of voices, birds, or cars; and tastes, if you are eating. You smell odors, possibly of food, perfume, soap, or newly cut grass. You receive touch sensations from this book, the chair on which you sit, and the floor that presses against your feet.

You perceive something when you become consciously aware of it by using one or more of your senses to receive stimuli from it. There are sense receptors that pick up information from your environment. The knowledge you acquire through your senses is called perception. However, as the next experiment reveals, what you perceive may be influenced by past experience. Furthermore, what you perceive may not be what it appears to be.

Materials:

- 3 large bowls
- tap water (hot, cold, and room temperature)
- ice cubes
- stopwatch, or clock or watch with second hand

There are sense receptors in your skin that respond to hot and cold. However, how you perceive temperature depends on the previous environment to which your sense receptors for temperature were exposed. This was first discovered by a German physiologist named Ernst Weber (1795–1878).

To begin this experiment, obtain three large bowls. To the first bowl add room-temperature tap water until the bowl is three-fourths full. Fill a second bowl about halfway with cold tap water. Add ice cubes until this bowl is also three-fourths full. Fill a third bowl to the same level with hot tap water. **As you add hot water to the bowl, test the water in the bowl with your hand. Be sure the water is not too hot. If it is, add some cold water until you are able to place your right hand in the water without discomfort.**

Place the three bowls side by side with the hot water on your right, the ice water on your left, and the room-temperature water in the middle. Dry your hands thoroughly. Then place your right hand in the hot water and your left hand in the ice water. Hold them under the water for three minutes.

After three minutes, remove your hands from the bowls and put both of them into the bowl of room-temperature water. How does your right hand perceive the water's temperature? How does your left hand perceive the water's temperature?

What does this experiment tell you about the way past experiences influence your perception of temperature?

Science Fair Project Idea

Place a large wooden object and a large metallic object side by side in the same room for an hour so that you know both objects are at the same temperature. Now touch first one object and then the other. Why do you think you perceive their temperatures to be different?

Chapter 4

Human Genetics

WE WILL NOW TURN OUR ATTENTION TO HEREDITY, GENETICS, AND DNA. Heredity is the transmission of characteristic traits, such as eye, hair, and skin color, from generation to generation. Genetics is the science that explores how those traits are passed from parents to offspring. As you will find, genes make up the chromosomes found in the nuclei of egg and sperm cells. They are the mechanisms for transmitting the information needed for new offspring to develop their characteristic traits. They also provide the codes that direct the many chemical and physical changes needed to maintain life. Chemically, genes are made of DNA (deoxyribonucleic acid), the blueprint from which organisms are made and that regulates all life processes.

Humans are unique in many ways. We make large-scale use of tools, we can control fire, we share food, we find or build protective shelters, and we transmit more than genes to our offspring. Because of our extensive use of language, we transmit beliefs and ideas from generation to generation. All these factors are parts of the main human advantage over other species, which is culture and the social structure that accompanies it. But culture seems to be the result of two things: a highly developed language and a large brain. It is doubtful that we ever had one without the other. Associated with culture, and perhaps also with language, brain size, and the capacity to convey ideas with symbols, is art. In fact, art, in the form of the drawings and paintings found in ancient cave dwellings, may have been our first attempt to convey ideas by the use of symbols.

The physical traits that characterize humans must be inherited because we find them persisting through many generations. But language, art, tools, the shelters we build, and the way we organize families and behave toward one another are not inherited. They differ from culture to culture. For example, many American Indian tribes were nomadic. They followed their food sources and built shelters that could be moved easily from place to place. The Europeans who came to America were predominantly farmers. They built permanent shelters and raised crops, cattle, pigs, and sheep near their shelters on land they claimed to own. The American Indians had no concept of owning land. It was not part of their culture.

Since the dawn of agriculture some ten thousand years ago, some human cultures have tried to improve the heredity of the domestic plants and animals they use for food. They did this by selecting the best organisms for breeding. Knowing that offspring resemble their parents, they selected for mating the goats that produced the most milk, the cattle that provided the most meat or milk, and the corn that produced the largest ears. Over centuries, their selective breeding led to plants and animals that were more productive. In some cases, however, particularly when the animals they bred were closely related, the results were unsatisfactory: The offspring were born dead or sickly. It took nearly ten millennia for people to understand why selective breeding worked in some cases and not in others.

EARLY THEORIES OF HEREDITY

More than twenty-five hundred years ago, Pythagoras (ca 580–ca 500 B.C.), an early Greek philosopher also known for his work in mathematics, tried to explain the transmission of characteristics. He argued that the hereditary traits of all animals, including humans, are carried in the male's semen. According to Pythagoras, semen, once inside the female's uterus, developed into a baby during gestation (the length of a pregnancy).

Two centuries later, Aristotle (384–322 B.C.), another Greek philosopher, reasoned that because children resemble their mothers as well as their fathers, both males and females must contribute hereditary factors. He believed that both sexes produce semen, which is derived from their blood. According to Aristotle, male and female semen unite in the uterus to form an embryo that grows into a baby during gestation.

Later, people believed that each body organ provided semen with "vapors" that contained the hereditary factors for that body part. However, in the seventeenth century, Antonie van Leeuwenhoek (1632–1723), while looking at semen through his simple microscope, saw sperm cells, or what he called animalcules. His discovery led people to believe that sperm transmit hereditary factors from father to offspring.

Others who examined sperm cells through microscopes claimed to see miniature humans—homunculi—curled up inside the sperm. This led to the belief that babies existed in a preformed state within sperm cells. In the warm and nourishing environment of the womb, these preformed embryos simply grew larger before being born.

At about the same time, others dissected animals and found swollen bodies on the ovaries of the females. These were correctly assumed to be eggs. This suggested that females transmit hereditary factors through their eggs, while males transmit theirs through sperm cells.

Pierre-Louis de Maupertuis (1698–1759) recognized that offspring often have physical characteristics that resemble those found in one or both parents. He proposed that tiny particles from all parts of the bodies of both parents are brought together at the time of conception. However, the factor for a particular feature from one parent, such as height or eye color, may dominate (hide) the corresponding factor from the other parent.

At about the time of the American Revolution, a German biologist, Caspar Friedrich Wolff (1734–1794), was studying chick embryos and other embryonic tissues under the microscope. He saw that no miniature versions of adult organs were present in an embryo. Over time, he observed that the unspecialized cells in an embryo change into muscle, nerve, blood, connective, and epithelial tissues. Wolff's work suggested that a sperm and an egg cell unite to form a single cell, a zygote (from the Greek word for yoked, or joined). The zygote then divides many times, forming a many-celled embryo. Eventually the cells become specialized, giving rise to tissues and organs that mature prior to birth.

Although Wolff's theory of embryonic development (epigenesis) was essentially correct, it was 1839 before it became widely accepted. By then, two German scientists, botanist Matthias Schleiden (1804–1881) and zoologist Theodor Schwann (1810–1882), had demonstrated that the cell is the fundamental unit of life in both plants and animals.

GREGOR MENDEL, THE FATHER OF GENETICS

By the middle of the nineteenth century, the idea that a sperm and egg cell combine to form a zygote that develops into a new organism during gestation had become widely accepted. However, the way hereditary traits are transmitted from one generation to the next remained a mystery.

Charles Darwin (1809–1882) wrote that evolution occurs because the great variety among members of a species makes some better suited for survival than others. However, he could not explain why organisms differ. Nor could he explain how traits are passed on from generation to generation.

It was Gregor Mendel (1822–1884), an Austrian monk, who first did experiments that led to the basic laws of genetics. Mendel, a botanist who was also trained in mathematics, began growing pea plants in the garden at his monastery in 1856. This was three years before Darwin published his book *On the Origin of Species*.

MENDEL'S INITIAL EXPERIMENTS

Mendel investigated, one at a time, seven traits he had observed in pea plants. These traits were height (tall or short), seed shape (round or wrinkled), color of the seed leaves or cotyledons (yellow or green), seed coats (clear or brown), pod shape (inflated or constricted), pod color (yellow or green), and position of pods on the stem (terminal or axial). Terminal pods form at the top of the stem, axial pods form along the sides of the stem. Figure 21 illustrates these traits.

Mendel began his experiments with true-breeding varieties—plants that had for many generations showed only one of the two forms for any of the seven traits he studied. He crossed (mated) true-breeding plants with plants of contrasting traits. These plants were known as the parent, or P_1, generation. To make these crosses, he carefully removed the

[FIGURE 21]

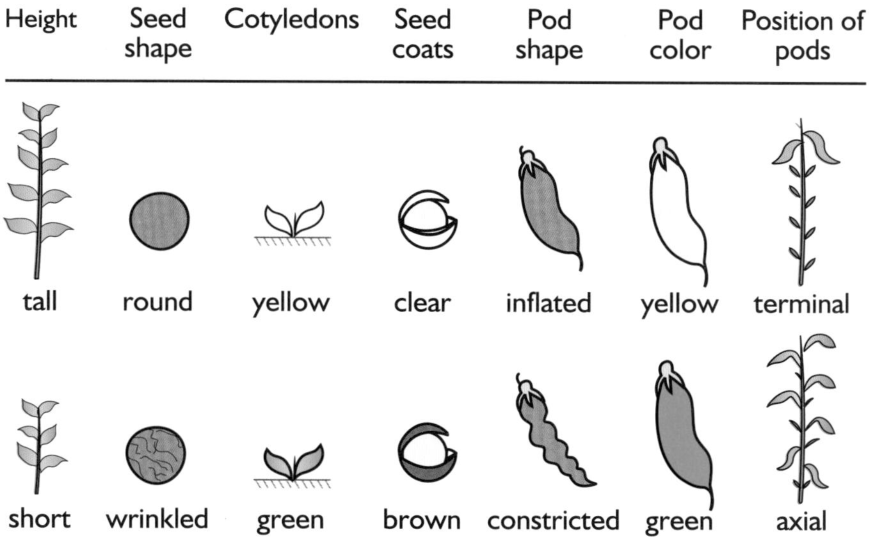

Height	Seed shape	Cotyledons	Seed coats	Pod shape	Pod color	Position of pods
tall	round	yellow	clear	inflated	yellow	terminal
short	wrinkled	green	brown	constricted	green	axial

The seven traits found in pea plants that were investigated by Gregor Mendel are illustrated in these drawings.

stamens from the flowers of, for example, a tall plant and placed their pollen on the pistils of a short plant. He also removed the stamens from the flowers of short plants and placed their pollen grains on the pistils of tall plants. This prevented the plants from self-pollinating, which is normally the way pea plants reproduce. He would then cover the flowers to prevent any further pollination by wind or insects.

The seeds produced by the cross-pollinated flowers from the P_1 generation were planted and observed. The plants that grew from these seeds—known as the first filial, or F_1, generation—flowered and were allowed to self-pollinate. The seeds produced by the F_1 generation grew into the plants of the second filial, or F_2, generation.

MENDEL'S RESULTS

When the P_1 generation was true-breeding tall plants crossed with true-breeding short plants, all the F_1 plants that grew from their seeds were tall. There were no short plants. However, the factor for shortness had not disappeared. When he allowed the F_1 plants to self-pollinate and produce the F_2 generation, the results were striking. Both tall and short plants grew from these seeds. The factor for shortness that had been hidden in the F_1 generation reappeared in one fourth of the F_2 plants. The other three fourths were tall, a ratio of 3:1.

When the plants of the F_2 generation reproduced by self-pollination, Mendel found that all the short plants were true-breeding: They produced only short offspring. Of the tall plants, one third were true-breeding; they produced only tall offspring. The other two thirds produced both tall and short plants in the same ratio (3:1) as their F_1 ancestors. Table 4 summarizes Mendel's results.

TABLE 4

Mendel's results when he crossed true-breeding tall pea plants with true-breeding short pea plants (P_1 generation), and then allowed their offspring to self-pollinate

Generation	Cross		Offspring from Seeds
P_1	tall × short	→	F_1—all tall
F_1	tall × tall	→	F_2—3 tall: 1 short
F_2	short × short	→	F_3—all short
	1/3 (tall × tall)	→	F_3—all tall
	2/3 (tall × tall)	→	F_3—3 tall: 1 short

Mendel found similar results when he crossed plants for each of the other six contrasting traits he studied. His results for the F_1 and F_2 generations for each of the seven traits he studied are shown in Table 5. In all cases, the F_2 plants produced the same 3:1 pattern of offspring.

The results show that in the F_2 generation, one trait is three times as likely to appear as the other. The trait that appears three times as frequently is the same one that appears in all plants in the F_1 generation. Mendel referred to the trait that appeared three times more frequently in

TABLE 5

Mendel's results for the F₁ and F₂ generations for each of seven traits inherited by pea plants. An ✕ is used to indicate a cross (mating) between plants with contrasting traits, such as tallness and shortness.

P_1	F_1	F_2	Ratio
tall ✕ short	all were tall	787 were round 277 were short	2.84:1
round ✕ wrinkled seeds	all were round	5,474 were round 1,850 were wrinkled	2.96:1
yellow ✕ green cotyledons	all were yellow	6,022 were yellow 2,001 were green	3.01:1
brown ✕ clear seed coats	all were brown	705 were brown 224 were clear	3.15:1
inflated ✕ constricted pods	all were inflated	882 were inflated 299 were constricted	2.95:1
green ✕ yellow pods	all were green	428 were green 152 were yellow	2.82:1
axial ✕ terminal pods	all were axial	651 were axial 207 were terminal	3.14:1

the F₂ generation as the dominant trait. A trait that disappeared in the F₁ generation, such as shortness, he called a recessive trait. When both traits were present in a seed, only the dominant one could be seen. It took precedence over the recessive trait. Thus, in pea plants, tallness is a dominant trait, while shortness is a recessive trait. From Table 5, can you identify the dominant and recessive trait in each of the other six characteristics Mendel investigated?

Mendel published the results of his experiments in 1866. His work was ignored. Biologists at that time were engrossed in Darwin's theory of evolution and paid attention to little else. Furthermore, many biologists who did read Mendel's paper were confused by his mathematical analysis of data.

In 1900, Hugo de Vries (1848–1935), a Dutch botanist, rediscovered Mendel's paper. De Vries, who had studied the inherited traits of primroses, was searching the literature for similar studies when he found Mendel's paper. He quickly realized that he had reached the same conclusions as had Mendel.

But de Vries's work went beyond Mendel's. He observed that every once in a while a new variety of primrose that differed significantly from others would suddenly appear and reproduce. De Vries had discovered the underlying cause of evolution. The sudden appearance of new traits were called mutations (from the Latin word *mutare*, meaning "to change"). Experiments demonstrated that a mutation that appeared in one member of a species could be transmitted to its offspring. If the change provided organisms with an adaptation that enabled them to better cope with their environment, then they were more likely to survive than other members of the species. Over time, the accumulation of mutations could lead to a new species. Mendel had discovered the basic manner in which traits are transmitted from generation to generation. De Vries had discovered mutations, the explanation for variation within a species that Darwin had sought.

CHROMOSOMES AND GENES

As microscopes improved, biologists began to observe details inside plant and animal cells. Most cells contained a spherical object that came to be known as the nucleus. Surrounding the nucleus was the jellylike cytoplasm. And while the cytoplasm of muscle, nerve, connective, blood, and epithelial cells was quite different, the nuclei of these cells appeared to be similar.

In 1879, Walther Flemming (1843–1905), a German anatomist, found that material within the nuclei of cells readily absorbed a red dye he was using to stain cells. He called this stringlike material chromatin, from the Greek word for color (*chroma*). By adding the dye to growing tissue, he could examine the chromatin at different stages of cell division. He found that as a cell began to divide, the chromatin became shorter and thicker, forming what came to be known as chromosomes ("colored bodies"). Flemming was able to observe the chromosomes at different stages of cell division, a process he called mitosis.

During the process, the stringlike chromatin winds into short, thick structures called chromosomes. The membrane surrounding the nucleus breaks down, and thin fibers known as spindle fibers form and attach to the chromosomes. As Figure 22 shows, each chromosome replicates (copies itself) so that the number of chromosomes doubles. The duplicates are then separated as they are pulled to opposite sides of the cell; two new cells form, each having the same number of chromosomes as the parent cell.

Biologists who studied mitosis were puzzled. If gametes have the same number of chromosomes as other cells, the zygotes formed by the union of sperm and egg cells would have twice as many chromosomes as their parents. Since all the cells of an organism appeared to come from the repeated mitotic division of the zygote, the number of chromosomes in the cells would double in each successive generation.

Careful observations of the cell divisions that occur during the formation of gametes provided an answer. Gametes, unlike other cells, are formed by a different type of cell division—a process that came to be known as meiosis, from a Greek word meaning "to diminish." During meiosis, only one member of each pair of chromosomes reaches a sperm or egg cell (see Figure 23). Consequently, the number of chromosomes in the gametes is half the number found in other cells. When gametes unite to form a zygote, the chromosomes pair up again, and the number of chromosomes per cell is restored to the number typical of the species. For humans, that number is 46 (23 pairs).

The discovery of chromosomes provided biologists with the actual matter that could transmit inherited traits from parents to offspring. The chromosomes were believed to be made up of smaller chemical units, called genes, which were the source of all inherited traits. The factors for the yellow or green color of peas, the height of the pea plants, the color of human eyes, and all other inherited characteristics were transmitted by genes found along the chromosomes in the nuclei of gametes.

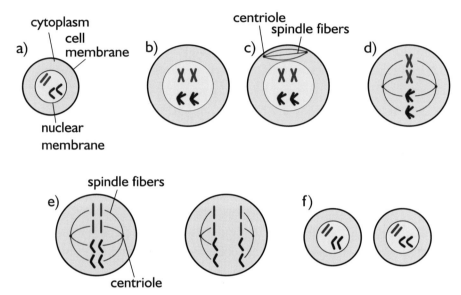

[FIGURE 22]

Mitosis is the splitting of a cell's nucleus during cell division. As a result of mitosis, each daughter cell has the same number and type of chromosomes as the parent cell. Before a cell begins mitosis, the genetic material is replicated. This diagram shows a cell with two pairs of chromosomes. a) A cell before mitosis. b) Each chromosome is made up of two sister chromatids. c) The nuclear membrane disappears; spindle fibers form. d) Spindle fibers attach to chromosomes lined up in the center of the cell. e) The chromosomes separate and sister chromatids move to opposite side of the cell. f) The cytoplasm of the cell divides, and two daughter cells form, each with the same number of chromosomes as the parent cell.

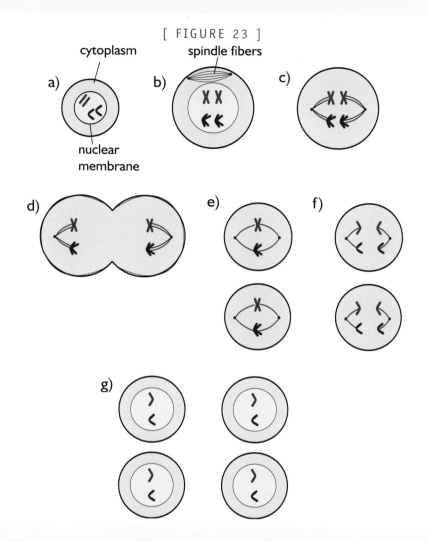

[FIGURE 23]

During meiosis each gamete receives only one member of each pair of chromosomes found in other cells of the body. Human cells have 46 chromosomes (23 pairs). Human sperm and egg cells have 23 chromosomes (one from each pair). As in mitosis, the genetic material is replicated before meiosis begins. a) The parent cells that give rise to gametes have the typical number of chromosomes for that species. This diagram shows a cell with two pairs of chromosomes. b) The nuclear membrane disappears and spindle fibers form. c) The chromosomes line up in homologous pairs on the cell's equator. d) One pair of each of the homologous pairs of chromosomes goes to opposite sides of the cell. The cell then divides, forming two daughter cells, each with two chromosomes (half the number that the parent cell had). e) Chromosomes in the daughter cells line up and are attached to spindle fibers. f) Each chromosome separates and sister chromatids move to opposite sides of the cell. g) The cells divide and a total of four cells, each with two chromosomes, have formed. These cells will become gametes.

Materials:

- prepared slides of mitosis and meiosis (available from biological supply company)
- microscope

Obtain microscope slides that have been stained to reveal different stages of mitosis and meiosis. The most commonly used cells are from onions, ascarids (roundworms), and whitefish. You may be able to borrow such slides and a microscope from your school's science department. A biology teacher might be willing to show you how to prepare such slides yourself.

Examine slides of mitosis. Can you see cells in which there is a distinct nuclear membrane and strands of chromatin? If you can, you are observing a cell that was not yet undergoing cell division. This step in cell division is called interphase. Cells in which the nuclear membrane disappears and spindle fibers are evident are in prophase. If you see chromosomes lined up near the cell's equator and attached to the spindle fibers, the cell is in metaphase. Can you see spindle fibers during metaphase? Can you detect cells where the chromosomes are separating and being pulled to opposite sides of the cell? These cells are in anaphase. In the last phase of cell division, known as telophase, the chromosomes are clustered at opposite sides of a cell and a new cell membrane is forming between them. The result is two

Science Fair Project Ideas

- Investigate how you might use an onion root tip to prepare a slide that would reveal various stages of cells undergoing mitosis. Then examine these slides under a microscope.
- Investigate how you might use an anther from a lily flower to prepare a slide that would reveal various stages of cells undergoing meiosis. Then examine these slides under a microscope.

daughter cells. What differences would you expect to find between cells undergoing mitosis as compared with those undergoing meiosis? Can you detect any such differences?

HEREDITY AND FAMILY

Understanding human genetics is fascinating but often difficult. Many human traits are inherited, but they cannot be investigated experimentally. Geneticists cannot require a man with curly black hair and green eyes to marry a woman who has straight red hair and brown eyes. These scientists must look for people with particular characteristics who have married and had children. Furthermore, people often dye their hair, even change their eye color, so that their natural traits may be hidden. In addition, humans have relatively few offspring; most human characteristics are the result of more than one pair of genes; and many traits, such as height and weight, are affected by environmental factors. For example, even though a person possesses genes for normal size, he or she may be short and frail because of poor nutrition. Much of what geneticists know about human inheritance comes from interviewing people and drawing a family tree (a pedigree) to try to figure out how a trait is inherited.

A FAMILY TREE

In drawing a family tree, females are represented by circles, males by squares. A horizontal line connecting a circle and a square represents a marriage. It can be called a marriage line. A short vertical line leading downward from the marriage line connects to a second horizontal line. This line has short vertical lines beneath it that lead to the circles and squares representing their children.

Figure 24a shows two married people, A and B, and their children X, Y, and Z. Figure 24b shows that A and B were the children of parents L and M, N and O, who are the grandparents of X, Y, and Z. Figure 24c reveals that these grandparents had other children—U and V and R, S,

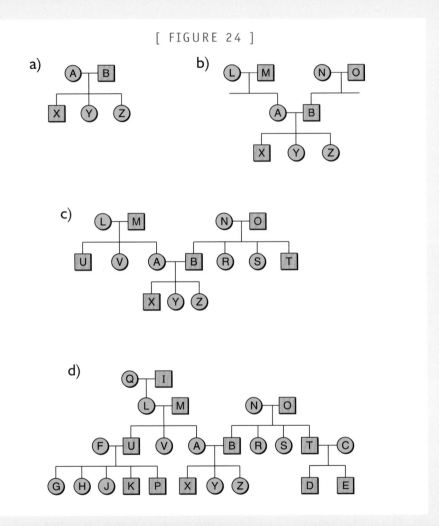

[FIGURE 24]

24a) A pedigree (family tree) showing the offspring from a marriage of A and B. Squares represent males; circles represent females. b) Branches have been added to show the parents of A and B (the grandparents of X, Y, and Z). c) The sibling lines have been extended to show the brothers and sisters of A and B. d) The children of siblings U and T have been added. The parents of L (Q and I, who are the grandparents of A and great-grandparents of X, Y, and Z) have also been added.

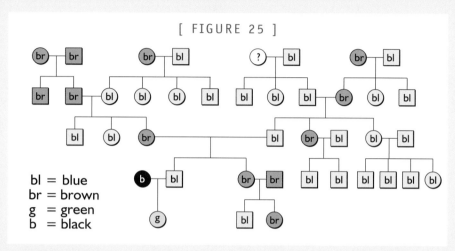

[FIGURE 25]

bl = blue
br = brown
g = green
b = black

A pedigree of a family that shows the eye color of most members of the family.

and T. U and V are A's siblings; R, S, and T are B's siblings. In Figure 24d, we learn that A's brother, U, married F, and they had five children, G, H, J, K, and P. B's brother, T, married C, and they had two children, D and E. We also discover that L was the only child of Q and I.

Notice that all members of the same generation are placed on the same horizontal level. This makes it easy to see that X, Y, and Z are the first cousins of G, H, J, K, and P, as well as D and E.

Once you have drawn as much of a family's pedigree as possible, you can begin to look for traits that have been transmitted from one generation to the next. If a person on the family tree is dead or living too far away to be observed, you will have to rely on his or her descendants to provide information about that person's phenotype. For example, the author's family tree, shown in Figure 25, can be used to trace eye color. A key is provided so that individuals and their eye color can be identified quickly.

In some instances, the genetics of a trait is well understood. In those cases, the genotype or genotype possibilities of a family member can be determined by knowing the phenotypes of his or her closest

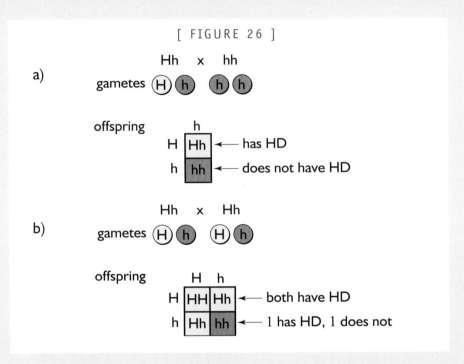

[FIGURE 26]

a)

Hh   x   hh

gametes (H)(h)   (h)(h)

offspring

	h
H	Hh	← has HD
h	hh	← does not have HD

b)

Hh   x   Hh

gametes (H)(h)   (H)(h)

offspring

	H	h
H	HH	Hh	← both have HD
h	Hh	hh	← 1 has HD, 1 does not

26a) Huntington's disease (HD) is carried by a rare dominant gene, H. If one parent has the gene, he or she will be affected and the children will have a 50:50 chance of inheriting the disease. b) If both parents have HD, the chances are 3:1 that the offspring will inherit the disease.

relatives. For example, Huntington's disease (HD), a severe debilitating affliction that attacks people after age thirty, is known to be carried by a rare dominant gene. If someone has the disease, he or she is most likely heterozygous because the gene is rare. If he or she has children with an unaffected person, their offspring stand a 50:50 chance of inheriting the disorder because they have an equal chance of receiving either the dominant or the recessive gene from the affected parent. The parent without the disease will transmit only the recessive gene (see Figure 26a). In the highly unlikely case that both parents have the disease, their offspring's chances of inheriting the disorder are 3:1 (see Figure 26b).

4.2 Making Your Own Family Tree

Materials:
- paper, preferably lined or graph paper
- pencil
- family members

To make your family tree, use lined paper and a pencil, because you will probably have to redraw the tree at least once. Draw the symbol that represents you (a square or a circle) near the center of the paper. Put your initials inside. Add your siblings if you have any, and write their initials inside the squares or circles. Add a vertical line upward to another horizontal line that connects your parents. On the same level as your parents, add your aunts and uncles and, if they are married, the people to whom they are married. Their children (your cousins) should be on the same level as you and your siblings. Where should you place your grandparents on this family tree? How about your great-grandparents? Is there enough information (ask your parents) to add your great-great-grandparents to the family tree? How about your great-great-great-grandparents? How many people have you placed on your family tree?

Keep the family tree you have made. It will be useful in the experiments that follow.

 Science Fair Project Ideas

- Make additions to your family tree as new people join your family through marriage or birth. If you keep it long enough, you can add your own children and your nieces and nephews to the tree.
- If small photographs are available, you could make an enlarged family tree with photographs in place of circles and squares.

Materials: →
- phenylthiocarbamide (PTC) paper strips (available from school biology department or from a science supply company)

- as many related people as possible from your family and other families

- pen or pencil

- notebook

About 70 percent of the American population can taste a chemical commonly known as PTC (phenylthiocarbamide). A solution of the chemical can be used to saturate paper strips that can be dried and preserved. When some people chew a strip of PTC paper, they sense a definite taste.

Place a strip of PTC paper in your mouth and chew it. Discard the paper after you have chewed it for a short time. Are you a taster or a nontaster? If you are a taster, describe the taste of PTC. Does it taste sweet, sour, bitter, or salty? If you are a nontaster, ask other people to chew a strip of the paper until you find a taster. How does a taster describe the taste of PTC?

Continue to test as many people as possible from different generations of your family and other families. Record your results and be sure to indicate the relationship among the people you test. Based on all the data you have collected, prepare family trees to show how the gene is transmitted through generations. Based on the pedigree, can you decide whether the ability to taste PTC is the result of a dominant or a recessive gene?

If you obtained results like those shown in Figure 27a, what might you conclude about the gene that transmits the ability to taste PTC? Would you change your mind on the basis of the data provided by the table in Figure 27b.

for PTC Tasting

[FIGURE 27a]

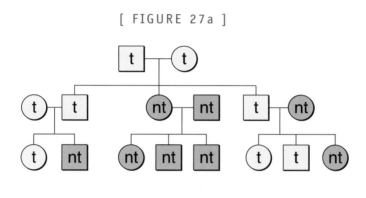

[FIGURE 27b]

Parents	Children	
	tasters	nontasters
taster x taster	450	60
taster x nontaster	230	215
nontaster x nontaster	0	98

In the family history shown in (a), tasters (people who can taste PTC) are represented by a t; nontasters are represented by nt. The data table provided in (b) is from a study of many families. Based on the data provided, do you think the ability to taste PTC is transmitted by a dominant or by a recessive gene? Why?

Materials:

-as many related people as possible from your family and other families

-pen or pencil

-notebook

CLEFT CHIN

Cleft chin (see Figure 28a) is believed to be the result of a dominant gene. Collect data from your own and/or other families where some family members have a cleft chin. Does your data support the idea that cleft chin is caused by a dominant gene? If not, what does it indicate?

DIMPLES

Dimples (see Figure 28b), too, are believed to be the result of a dominant gene. Collect data from your own and/or other families where some of the people have dimples. Does your data support the idea that dimples are caused by a dominant gene? If not, what does it indicate?

ROLLED TONGUE

The ability to roll your tongue lengthwise (see Figure 28c) is believed to be the result of yet another dominant gene. Collect data from your own and/or other families where some family members are able to roll their tongues. Does your data support the idea that this ability is the result of a dominant gene? If not, what does it indicate?

EARLOBES

Earlobes can be free or attached (see Figure 28d). Collect data from your own and/or other families where some family members have free earlobes and others have attached earlobes. Does either trait appear to be the result of a dominant gene? If not, what, if anything, does your data indicate about the inheritance of this trait?

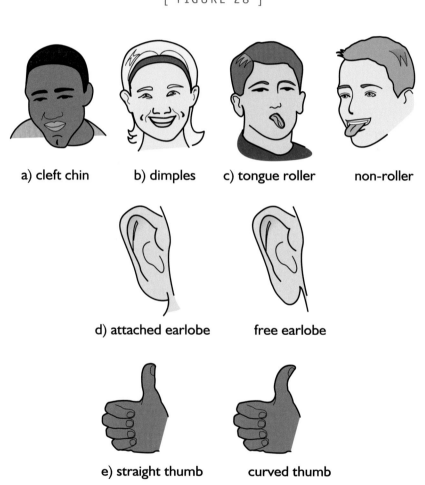

[FIGURE 28]

a) cleft chin   b) dimples   c) tongue roller   non-roller

d) attached earlobe   free earlobe

e) straight thumb   curved thumb

A number of readily visible characteristics are inherited.

THUMB SHAPE

As shown in Figure 28e, extended thumbs can be straight or curved. Collect data from your own and/or other families where some of the people have straight thumbs and others have curved thumbs. Does either trait appear to be the result of a dominant gene? If not, what, if anything, does your data indicate about the inheritance of this trait?

HUMAN BLOOD TYPES

Human blood is of different types. Red blood cells may carry a substance called an antigen. Antigens, known as A and B, are chemical compounds that, when present, cause antibodies to form. These antibodies, known as anti-A and anti-B, react with a specific antigen. The anti-A antibody reacts with the A antigen; the anti-B antibody reacts with the B antigen.

An individual's red blood cells may contain one, both, or neither of the two antigens. Human blood, therefore, can be one of four types: A, B, AB, or O. As you can see from Table 6, a person with type A blood has the A antigen on his or her red blood cells; a person with type B blood has the B antigen; someone with type AB blood has both antigens; and a person with type O blood has neither antigen. Blood serum (the fluid part of blood that remains after blood clots) may contain antibodies that react with the A or B antigens, causing the blood cells to clump together (agglutinate). Agglutination can be seen through a microscope. Consequently, a person's blood type can be readily determined.

As you can see from Table 6, a person with type AB blood has neither antibody. If she did, her antibodies would react with the antigens on her own red blood cells, causing agglutination. Agglutinated cells would be unable to flow through small blood vessels and the person would die.

To determine a person's blood type, a small amount of his or her blood is placed on each of two glass slides. A drop of blood serum containing the anti-A antibody is added to one drop; a drop of serum containing the anti-B antibody is added to the other drop. As Table 7 reveals, either anti-A or anti-B will cause type AB blood to clump. On the other hand,

TABLE 6

The four blood types and the antigens on their red blood cells (RBC) and the antibodies in their blood serum

Blood type	Antigens on RBC	Antibodies in serum
A	A	Anti-B
B	B	Anti-A
AB	A and B	Neither antibody
O	Neither antigen	Anti-A and Anti-B

TABLE 7

Typing blood by adding a known antiserum to the blood in question. A plus sign (+) indicates agglutination; a minus sign (-) indicates no agglutination.

Anti-A serum added to the blood sample	Anti-B serum added to the blood sample	Test indicates antigen on the RBC is:	Test indicates antigen on the RBC is:
+	-	A	A
-	+	B	B
+	+	A and B	AB
-	-	neither	O

a person with type O blood carries both antibodies but neither antigen on his red blood cells. Therefore, his blood cells will not clump when blood serum with either antibody is added. Someone with type A blood has the A antigen and the anti-B antibodies. Her red blood cells will clump when anti-A serum is added but not when anti-B serum is added. Type B blood, which contains the B antigen, will clump when anti-B serum is added but not when anti-A serum is added.

The percentages of white and black people in the United States with each of the four blood types are found in Table 8. As you can see, type O is the most common, type AB the most rare, and the frequency of each type is related to race.

In addition to the A, B, AB, and O blood types, humans possess other blood antigens for which tests have been developed. For example, people may be either Rh positive (85%) or Rh negative (15%); they may be type M, type N, or type MN.

Considering all the possible combinations of blood types and enzymes, an individual may be quite unique. For example, the probability of having both type AB and Rh negative blood is $0.04 \times 0.15 = 0.006$ or 6 people in a thousand. If other blood factors are considered, the probability of finding someone with identical blood may be extremely small.

TABLE 8

The four blood types and the frequency of their occurrence in two races of Americans

Blood Type	American Whites (%)	American Blacks (%)
O	45	49
A	40	27
B	11	20
AB	4	4

Materials:

- as many related people as possible from your family and other families

- pen or pencil

- notebook

Because blood tests are so common, most people know their blood type. Someone who tells you he is O-negative has blood that is type O and Rh negative. Obtain the blood types of as many people who are related to one another as possible. Start with your own family. What is your blood type? What are the blood types of your brothers and sisters? What are or were your parents' blood types? Your grandparents? Your great-grandparents? Record all your data. It should include the blood type (O, A, B, or AB; and Rh positive or negative) of each person and the relationships of the people involved.

Then investigate the blood types of other people who are related. Record all that data as well.

One investigation might provide data like that found in the family tree shown in Figure 29. What if anything can you conclude about the inheritance of blood type from the evidence in the table? Does any of the data in Figure 29 conflict with yours?

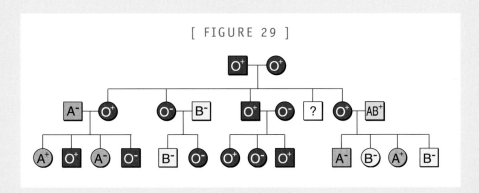

[FIGURE 29]

A family tree showing blood types—A, B, AB, and O; Rh+ or Rh−.

Geneticists who have studied the inheritance of blood types among humans have found that if both parents are Rh negative, all their children will be Rh negative. In some marriages where both parents are Rh positive, all the children are Rh positive. In other such marriages, some of their offspring are Rh negative. In some marriages where one parent is Rh positive and the other Rh negative, all the children are Rh positive. In other such marriages, some of the children are Rh positive and some are Rh negative. All this suggests that the gene for Rh positive blood is dominant to the gene for Rh negative blood.

TABLE 9

The inheritance of A, B, AB, and O blood types based on results from a large group of families

Blood Type of Parents	Blood Types that May Appear in Children	Blood Types that Will Not Appear in Children
O × O	O	A, B, AB
O × A	O, A	B, AB
O × B	O, B	A, AB
O × AB	A, B	O, AB
A × A	A, O	B, AB
A × B	O, A, B, AB	—
A × AB	A, B, AB	O
B × B	O, B	A, AB
B × AB	A, B, AB	O
AB × AB	A, B, AB	O

Other genetic studies reveal that if both parents have type O blood, all their children will have type O blood. Similarly, in some marriages where one parent has type A blood and the other has type O, all the children will have type A blood. In other such marriages, some children will have type A blood and some will have type O.

In some marriages where one parent has type B blood and the other has type O blood, all the children will have type B blood. In other such marriages, some children will have type B blood and some will have type O blood.

If a person with type AB blood marries a person with type O blood, their children will have either type A or type B blood. Table 9 summarizes the inheritance of A, B, AB, and O blood types. Does your data agree with the data in the table? Based on all the available data, see if you can explain how these blood types are inherited.

Science Fair Project Idea

Blood or bloodstains are often found at crime scenes. Usually the blood type can be determined readily. How might the blood type be used to show that a person suspected of the crime is innocent? Can it be used to prove a person is guilty?

Chapter 5

Personality, Learning, and Memory

YOUR PERSONALITY CONSISTS OF THOSE BEHAVIORS, CHARACTERISTICS, AND TRAITS by which you are recognized as an individual. It is the basis for your reputation, for the way others see you. The word *personality* comes from the Latin word *persona*, which means "mask." Your personality, based on the Latin, is the mask you present to the world. This implies that a person's outward behavior, which provides the impression he or she makes on others, may not be what the person is really like. In some cases this is true. We all know people who can "put it on." They are able to make a good first impression with teachers or at a social event where they meet important people, but within their family or among close friends, they may exhibit very different behavior.

BEHAVIORAL TRAITS

There are many behavioral traits that make up an individual's personality. Some people are very talkative and outgoing. They are called extroverts. Introverts, on the other hand, are quiet and reserved, even shy. Some people are optimistic about the world around them; others view it with pessimism. People may appear to be happy, sad, or passive. Some are aggressive; some are reserved. These and many other traits make up one's personality. But these traits are not constant. They can change depending on the situation. An extrovert may be quiet at a funeral, and introverts may be more outgoing with close friends. The behavioral traits that constitute a personality reflect a person's average behavior.

Beneath one's behavior are thoughts and feelings, the basis for the actions others observe. People who are empathetic—sensitive, compassionate, and kindhearted—reveal these feelings by their actions. They are supportive, attentive, and willing to listen to others. Their desire to help others is evident from their posture, tone of voice, and expression.

Some people, on the other hand, may fake such behavior in order to be liked or gain the approval of someone they think can help them achieve a goal. Still others may be truly empathetic but think that being helpful means solving problems and giving advice. As a result, they appear insensitive and overbearing to those they most want to help.

The healthiest mental condition belongs to the person whose behavior with others is the same as the feelings he or she has inside. For most of us, however, there are areas of our personality that are viewed differently by others than by ourselves. And there are secret aspects of our personalities that are known only to us and not to the rest of the world. Many believe there are also areas of the personality that remain in the unconscious mind and are known to no one.

PERSONALITY AND THE UNCONSCIOUS MIND

Many psychiatrists (doctors who treat mental disorders) contend that they can bring out thoughts hidden in the unconscious minds of their patients. They use projective tests to try to make contact with unconscious thoughts and desires. In the Rorschach test, for instance, the subject is asked to give his or her reaction to an inkblot. Since the patterns have no meaning, it is assumed that whatever is seen by the subject is the result of his or her unconscious thoughts.

PERSONALITY, THE BRAIN, AND CHEMISTRY

The brain is the source of all our thoughts and emotions. The personality traits that we exhibit originate in our brains, which are structured according to a pattern found in the genes we inherit. Some psychologists estimate that about half of our personality is the result of our genes.

Other parts of our personalities are molded by our environment and culture.

In recent years the chemicals released from brain cells have been identified and their effects on the body determined. The release of the chemical dopamine into the brain is associated with the outgoing, pleasure-seeking behavior characteristic of extroverts. Low levels of dopamine have the opposite effect. An enzyme, monoamine oxidase, counteracts dopamine, and high levels of this substance are characteristic of sedate personalities. Nerve impulses arising in the frontal lobe of the brain can inhibit the production of a substance called serotonin and cause impulsive behavior such as irritability, aggression, and violence.

The male sex hormone testosterone is believed to be the reason that aggressive behavior is more common in men than in women. It is mostly young men who engage in such contact sports as football, rugby, and hockey. It is also males who commit 90 percent of all violent crimes.

Among early humans, aggressive behavior from high levels of testosterone helped people survive. The males could hunt for food and drive off animal and human predators. Such aggressive behavior is far less important in today's world, where food is available in stores and national armies provide protection.

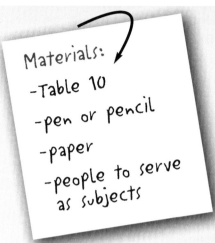

Materials:
- Table 10
- pen or pencil
- paper
- people to serve as subjects

Psychologists often give tests in an effort to determine an individual's personality. For example, questions can be designed to determine if a person is an extrovert or an introvert. Most people are somewhere in between. They are sometimes outgoing, sometimes shy or reserved, sometimes indifferent. A test to determine if a person is an extrovert or an introvert could be made from items such as those listed in Table 10.

How would you expect an extrovert to respond to each of these items? How would you expect an introvert to respond?

Add more items and questions of your own design in order to develop a test that will determine whether someone is an extrovert, introvert, or neither.

To find out if your test is useful in identifying extroverts and introverts, try it with people you know well.

If your test seems useful in identifying extroverts and introverts, try it on a number of people you do not know well. If it does not, try to change those items that are not useful and add new items that are effective in identifying these personality traits.

Science Fair Project Idea

Design and carry out a test to determine the strength of a person's self-esteem.

TABLE 10

There are several ways to test people to determine whether they are extroverts or introverts.

I. A number of paired statements are listed below. Circle the statement, a or b, that you feel best represents you.

1. a) I sometimes like to be alone.
   b) I do not like to be alone.
2. a) I prefer to have a few close friends.
   b) I prefer to have many casual friends.
3. a) I don't like it when people dare me to do something.
   b) I enjoy it when people dare me to do something.
4. a) I hate to sell things.
   b) I enjoy selling things.
5. a) If I were to be involved in a play, I'd prefer to build or design the props.
   b) If I were to be involved in a play, I'd want to be one of the actors on stage.

II. A number of statements are listed below. Answer each one by writing the response—A B, C, or D—that best fits you.

A. Strongly disagree   C. Agree to some extent
B. Disagree to some extent   D. Strongly agree

1. I see myself as talkative.
2. I see myself as reserved.
3. I see myself as enthusiastic about most things I do.
4. I see myself as sociable and outgoing.
5. I tend to reflect on most things before talking about them.

5.2 Revealing Inkblots

Materials:
- figure 30
- paper and pen
- ink
- as many people as possible

You read earlier that psychiatrists use the Rorschach test to try to reach a person's unconscious mind. The results of such a projective test can be properly interpreted only by someone trained in clinical psychology or psychiatry. You can do some reading in an encyclopedia or textbook or on the Internet about how subjects' responses reveal their mental state. You may find it interesting to ask people to look at inkblots, such as the one in Figure 30, and ask them what they see.

What do you see when you look at Figure 30? Ask as many people as possible, one at a time, to tell you what they see when they look at the figure. What do they say? Do any two or more people interpret the inkblot in the same way?

Make some inkblots of your own and ask people to tell you what they see. You can either design the shape of the inkblots or simply let ink fall on a piece of paper in a random way.

LEARNING AND MEMORY

Psychologists define *learning* as a relatively permanent change in behavior or knowledge resulting from experience. There are three basic types of learning: classical conditioning, operant conditioning, and cognitive learning. In classical conditioning a person learns by his response to an outside experience, a stimulus. In operant conditioning one learns from the results of behavior. In cognitive learning a person gets information by reasoning and thinking.

[FIGURE 30]

What do you see when you look at this inkblot?

Memory involves the encoding, storage, and retrieval of information and past experiences. Encoding involves organizing the information we take in. Storage is the process of retaining that information. Retrieval is the ability to recognize or recall what has been stored. We use memory to record events in our lives as well as the information and skills related to those experiences.

CLASSICAL CONDITIONING

Ivan Pavlov's research with dogs was the first scientific investigation of conditioning. Pavlov, working at the beginning of the twentieth century, placed meat powder on a dog's tongue to stimulate a reflex flow of saliva. If he rang a bell just before placing the meat powder on the tongue, the dog would soon begin to salivate at the sound of the bell even without the meat powder stimulus. Pavlov called the meat powder the unconditioned stimulus (UCS). It caused the unconditioned response (UCR)—saliva flow. At the beginning of this experiment, the neutral stimulus (NS), the bell, did not produce any response (NR). During conditioning, the bell was repeatedly presented just before the meat powder, the unconditioned stimulus, was placed on the dog's tongue. After conditioning, the bell became a conditioned stimulus (CS) that caused salivation as a conditioned response (CR) even if the unconditioned stimulus (meat powder) was not given. The equations below summarize the conditioning process.

$$UCS \rightarrow UCR$$
(meat powder)   (saliva flow)

$$NS \rightarrow NR$$
(bell)   (no response)

$$NS + UCS \rightarrow UCR$$
(bell)   (meat powder)   (saliva flow)

The neutral stimulus (bell) soon becomes a conditioned stimulus, so that

$$CS \rightarrow CR$$
(bell) (saliva flow)

5.3 Conditioning

Materials:
- several people to serve as subjects
- chair or table (high enough so feet are off ground)
- a friend
- rubber hammer or suitable substitute such as a stick inserted into a large one-hole rubber stopper
- paper
- pencil
- something to serve as a conditioned stimulus such as a pencil that can be tapped, or a bell

In classical conditioning a stimulus can produce a response that it would not normally cause. You can do an experiment in classical conditioning using the same knee response that a doctor uses to test reflexes. Carry out several trials with a subject. Ask your subject to sit on a chair or table high enough so that her feet are off the floor. Lightly tap her knee with the rubber hammer. Just before you tap her knee, a friend serving as your assistant can ring a bell or strike a table with a pencil. After a number of trials, the sound should produce the response without your having to strike the subject's leg with the rubber hammer. The subject is now reacting to a conditioned stimulus she hears, not to the unconditioned stimulus she feels.

How many trials do you think it will take before the sound becomes a conditioned stimulus? Try it out and see if your prediction is correct.

How might you eliminate the conditioned reflex? How many trials are needed before the conditioned stimulus no longer produces the conditioned response?

OPERANT CONDITIONING

B. F. Skinner (1904–1990) defined the term *operant conditioning* in the 1930s. Operant conditioning is a form of learning in which a behavior becomes more or less probable depending on its consequences. The behavior elicited depends on the consequences that follow. There are different types of consequences, but we will focus on positive reinforcement, which is the easiest to observe and the most ethical.

In positive reinforcement, there is an increase in the probability of a behavior that is followed by a desirable consequence. You probably know a teacher who gives stickers for good work or behavior. That would be an example of positive reinforcement. Another example is your parents' permission to let you watch television after you finish your homework. You are more likely to complete your homework if you know that a desirable activity will follow.

Animal trainers use positive reinforcement to train animals. For example, dogs do not normally jump through hoops. Trainers use a process called shaping to elicit the desired behavior. Shaping involves rewarding the subject for doing something related to the objective. Reinforcement follows performance of the desired conduct.

To train a dog to jump through a hoop, the trainer first rewards the dog for coming close to the hoop, then for stepping in the hoop, then for walking through the hoop, and finally for jumping through the hoop. Obviously, the desired behavior has to be one that the subject can perform. You could not train your dog to use a knife and fork to eat its food, but you could train it to "shake hands" or roll over. Make sure that you are consistent with your reinforcement and that it is working to condition your subject. Praise and small bits of food are positive reinforcers to a dog or other pet.

It will take many trials to train an animal to do a trick. And you must remember to take into consideration the animal's age. The old saying "You can't teach an old dog a new trick" is not necessarily true. However, if your dog is old or arthritic, do not try to teach it to do a trick that could be physically painful to perform. Also, a very young puppy may not be developmentally ready to learn the skill you want to establish. Furthermore, you must take into consideration the kind of animal you want to train. Some animals, such as dogs, are easier to train than others, such as rabbits.

COGNITIVE LEARNING AND MEMORY

Classical and operant conditioning are concerned with changing behavior. Cognitive learning is more closely associated with the acquisition of knowledge or information. This type of learning requires memory because acquired information is stored for retrieval in our brains. We use our memory to record our experiences and to gain information and skills from experience. Through our memory we can bring to mind an event or information from the past.

5.4 Maze Learning

Materials:

- several people to serve as subjects
- blindfold
- maze
- table
- chair
- stylus (swizzle stick or unsharpened pencil)
- stopwatch, or clock or watch with a second hand
- lined paper
- pencil

You have probably heard of psychologists' experimenting with a mouse running through a maze. The mouse tries to reach a reward by learning to run the maze through a series of trial-and-error explorations. People perform the same sort of trial-and-error explorations when learning new motor or verbal skills, such as riding a bicycle or reciting a poem. In this experiment you will find out how quickly people can learn to move successfully through a maze like the one shown in Figure 31.

You will need to test subjects individually. Of course, the subjects should not see the maze before the experiment. Blindfold the subject and seat him at a table in front of the maze. Put the stylus in his hand and place the stylus at the beginning of the maze, which he should note is a circle by moving the stylus. Inform him that the goal is a circular space similar to the starting position. Tell the subject he is being timed and there are paths that are dead ends. His goal is to maneuver through the maze as quickly as possible using only the hand that holds the stylus. Let the subject repeat his trip through the maze until he has made three trips without going into a dead end or turning the wrong way. Time each trip and keep track of the number of errors. Do not ask a subject to do more than twenty trials.

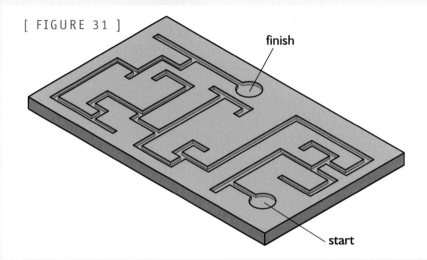

[FIGURE 31]

finish

start

A maze like the one shown in this drawing can be made from a board into which a grooved path is burned or cut. (A shop student or teacher may be able to help you make the maze.) A swizzle stick or an unsharpened pencil can serve as a stylus for "running" the maze.

Graph the results of the trials for each individual on a line graph. Have one graph show the time taken to complete the maze versus the number of previous trials. Another graph can show the number of errors versus the number of previous trials.

Does the time taken per trial and the number of errors decrease as the trials progress? Did subjects show steady improvement or were there trials where no improvement took place?

 Science Fair Project Ideas

- Design an experiment to find out whether the speed of learning to "run" the maze is related to the age of the participant.
- Design experiments to test other factors that might affect the rate at which people learn to move through the maze. For example, does age affect the rate?

5.5 Backward Alphabet

Materials:

- several people to serve as subjects
- lined sheets of paper numbered 1-10 for each subject
- pencils
- stopwatch, or clock or watch with a second hand

Learning new material for school or learning a new skill takes practice. You have to practice writing the words in a new spelling list; you have to practice to successfully do a flip in gymnastics. The old saying "Practice makes perfect" is true. But are there ways to practice that are better than others? Should you take a break and let the information soak in, or should you practice nonstop for an extended period? This experiment will help you answer such questions.

Ask a number of subjects to write the alphabet backward, from Z to A. Give them one minute to complete the task. Immediately after the minute has passed, ask them to do it again. Continue until they have completed ten trials.

Next, have a second group start the same way by writing the alphabet backward. After one minute, let them rest for a minute. Then ask them to write the alphabet backward again. Continue this sequence of writing and resting for ten trials. How do the results of the two groups compare?

How can you represent the results on a graph? Which group was more successful in completing the task? Did both groups continue to get better as the trials progressed?

Based on the results of your experiment, should you take a break and let the information soak in when learning a task or should you practice nonstop for an extended period?

Science Fair Project Ideas

- Design an experiment to find out if fatigue is a factor in learning to write the alphabet backward.
- Design an experiment to find out whether taking breaks or practicing nonstop is the better way to learn a physical activity.

Materials:
- several people
- pencils or pens
- paper

Active, or short-term, memory is the ability to remember something for a short time. You might guess that our ability to remember items, especially unrelated or meaningless details, is limited. In this experiment you will have an opportunity to test this assumption.

Gather a group of people and pass out paper and pencils to them. You will read a list of unrelated numbers to the group. Start with four digits and increase by one up to twelve digits. After you read the first group of four digits, immediately ask the group to write the digits you have read. They should not start to write until you have finished reading the group of digits. Repeat with the next group of five digits and continue with all the groups in the same manner. You can use the following list of digits or you can prepare your own list.

6 2 9 5
3 5 8 4 2
7 2 6 8 1 3
5 9 6 3 5 2 4
2 6 9 1 4 7 3 8
1 7 4 2 8 6 3 5 9
8 5 2 4 1 9 6 7 3 5
4 3 8 2 7 1 4 9 6 2 5
9 4 1 7 9 5 6 8 1 3 4 2

When checking the subjects' lists, all the numbers in a line must be in the correct order or that line is considered wrong. How many numbers can the average person immediately recall? It will probably be six or seven if your results are similar to other investigators'.

Were some participants better at remembering long lines of numbers than others? If there were such people, ask them if they know why they were able to remember the numbers.

THOUGHT AND THINKING

Psychologists define *thinking* as the ability to reason or reflect. We think every time we solve a problem, judge the truth of a statement, or consider the pros and cons of a situation before making a decision. To perform any of these actions we draw on what we already know. If a situation is one we have encountered before, we can employ the thought processes we used before. If the position we are in is unfamiliar but resembles others we have encountered, we can draw on more general knowledge. However, we are not always as rational and logical as we might think. Past experience and learning can influence and interfere with our thinking, as we will see.

Science Fair Project Idea

Design and carry out an experiment to find out if the rate at which you read the numbers affects a person's ability to remember them.

🏆 5.1 The Stroop Effect

Materials:
- pens with different colored ink
- paper
- stopwatch, or clock or watch with second hand
- several people to serve as subjects

Once we learn to read, we automatically read any words we see. Sometimes reading gets in the way of our thinking process because we cannot help reading even when we do not want to. The Stroop effect shows this problem with our thinking and how it can affect the speed at which we process information.

Print some nonsense letter groups in colored ink on paper. Some examples are given below. A suggested color for each letter group is given in parentheses. Have four columns of words twelve lines long. (We have provided possible sample letter groups for the first two lines. You will have to make up the next ten lines.) Also prepare a list of the colors of letter groups that you can use for checking. Use a stopwatch to determine how long it takes for the person to tell you the correct color of all the letter groups in the list.

PLG	WKN	WVD	BLG
TPY	ZMG	LHBF	QOX

This part of the experiment should move along quickly. What is the average time for a subject to state the colors of all the letter groups?

Now do the same thing using real words. Again, examples for the first two lines are provided. You will need to write the next ten.

SPOON	OAK	PONY	CHILD
TABLE	BABY	TOY	BELL

How long does it take for the average subject to correctly name, for all the words, the color of the ink in which each word is printed?

Now prepare lists of words that are the names of colors. However, print them in a different color than the word. Repeat the directions again at this point so that a subject clearly knows that he is to name the color of the ink used to print the word, not the word itself. Again, the first two lines are provided. You will have to write the next ten.

GREEN	BLUE	BROWN	RED
BROWN	RED	GREEN	BLUE

This part of the experiment will take longer than the other two parts because of the Stroop effect. Our brains naturally want to read the words and it will take some time before the thinking process will enable the subject to focus on the color of the ink rather than the word.

What was the average time for a subject to name the colors of the words in each of the first two trials? What was the average time for subjects to name the colors of the words in the last trial, where the words were the names of colors? How did the Stroop effect affect the speed at which the colors could be named?

 Science Fair Project Ideas

- Design and conduct an experiment to find out if the Stroop effect occurs with clusters of numbers in place of words. Suppose you had clusters of numbers in place of letters arranged in the same way as in Experiment 5.7. The subject should tell you how many numbers are in each cluster. For example, if the cluster is 777, the subject should say, "Three," not "Seven, seven, seven."
- You might also test for the Stroop effect when symbols are used in place of letters or numbers. Some examples are given below with the answers in parentheses.

(4) $$$ (3)   % % (2)   &&&&& (5)

Is the Stroop effect as powerful using symbols and numbers as it was using the names of colors?

FURTHER READING

Books

Harris, Elizabeth Snoke. *First Place Science Fair Projects for Inquisitive Kids*. New York: Lark Books, 2005.

Hawkes, Chris. *The Human Body: Uncovering Science*. Ontario, Canada: Firefly Books, 2006.

McMillan, Beverly. *Human Body: A Visual Guide*. Buffalo, N.Y.: Firefly Books, 2006.

Moorman, Thomas. *How to Make Your Science Project Scientific. Revised Edition*. New York: John Wiley & Sons, Inc., 2002.

Vecchione, Glen. *Blue Ribbon Science Projects*. New York: Sterling Pub. Co., 2005.

Internet Addresses

Kids Biology.com. 1998–2008.
http://www.kidsbiology.com/human_biology/index.php.

The Nemours Foundation. *Kids Health*. 1995–2008.
http://www.kidshealth.org/kid/

Society for Science and the Public. *Science News for Kids*. 2008.
http://www.sciencenewsforkids.org/

INDEX